HINDUISM
BENEATH THE SURFACE

A family's attempt to understand Sanatana Dharma

KANNAN KN

INDIA • SINGAPORE • MALAYSIA

DEDICATION

In loving memory of my parents

Appa (Shri R Narayanamoorthy)

and

Amma (Smt V L Janaki)

Contents

Foreword

[By Mr Arvind Sinha, a world-renowned documentary filmmaker, winner of eight National (President's) Awards and numerous highly prestigious international awards. Arvind was the Jury Chair for Non-Feature Films in IFFI 2023. His films have been showcased in the biggest and most important documentary events in the world. Arvind is also a keen student of Sanatana Dharma]

Kannan and I were classmates in school. Kannan did CA and CS and went into the corporate world and achieved success. I was nudged by destiny to become a filmmaker. Now we are actively connected through social media. Both of us realised that we have a common interest in religion and spirituality. It has been his concern that there isn't any material available in simple language and in brief that deals with the basics of Sanatana or Hindu philosophy. His concern is that our youngsters, in trying to be 'modern', aren't even aware of the basics of

Sanatana philosophy and practises. And in the process, they are missing out on the available tools of acquiring or reaching excellence in their lives. Most people aren't aware that religion and spirituality are the manual for the guidance of human life. They help one to understand life and to live it in the best possible manner. Religion and spirituality show us the art of living. The Bhagavad Gita is the greatest book of management for mankind. I too have a deep interest in Sanatana philosophy and practises. Kannan wrote the book and sent me the manuscript. It is in simple fiction form and covers the basics of Sanatana Dharma. It answers most of the questions that arise in the minds of the common Hindu, especially the young generation.

What does a man want? Man doesn't want *'dukha'* (pain and misery), he wants *'sukha'* (happiness). EVERY act of man from the moment he gets up to the moment he retires for the day is in search of happiness or *sukha*. Religion and spirituality provide us with the guidance in a systematic way to get happiness and ultimately attain permanent happiness or the experience of bliss - *parmananda*.

To make the book interesting, Kannan has given it a fictional form - of conversations within a modern educated Hindu family which includes a couple of youngsters. That's nice because most of our scriptures, including the Bhagavad Gita, are also in question-answer form. Kannan is precise and to the point, and going through this book will take only a few hours. It covers most of the aspects of Sanatana Dharma in brief. This book not only answers the questions that frequent the minds of most ordinary Hindus but will also get them interested to delve deeper into the subject. Kannan deftly leads the reader through the various topics of Sanatana Dharma or Hinduism as it's commonly called, namely 'Life's purpose', 'God and Godliness', 'Maya', 'Who am I', 'The Karma theory', 'Fate vs Freewill', the various paths to happiness - *Jnana* Yoga, *Bhakti* Yoga, *Karma* Yoga and *Raja* Yoga, Mind Management, *Daivi* and *Aasuri* qualities, Advaita, Vishishtadvaita, Dvaita, Varna and Caste, Ritualistic prayers and Practises etc.

Such a book is much needed. Wishing Kannan and this book all success.

Section A
Getting off to a Good Start

To truly benefit from a book on philosophy, it's important to be clear at the very outset about what one is looking for from the book. This section would help the readers frame that purpose and set both their approach and expectations while embarking on this journey.

To make it more relatable, the book's content has been presented through everyday conversations within a fictional family. This section also introduces the reader to the characters within this family.

Chapters in this Section

1. **Why did I Write this book?**
2. **Why Should you Read this Book?**
3. **A Turmoil in the Rajan Household**

Chapter 1

Why Did I Write This Book?

"Why do we have so many Gods in Hinduism?"
asks the teenager, and the parent draws a blank!

I am a Hindu. I was born in Kolkata to Tamil Brahmin parents. My seven siblings and I were raised in a family environment of Sanatana Dharma. My father, an engineer, was a spiritual seeker, while my mother was deeply religious. They had integrated their respective spiritual and religious practises seamlessly into their daily lives. However, neither of them ever forced me to pray or follow any ritual or practice.

After completing my university and professional education (ACA/ACS), I went into an almost single-minded pursuit of a professional career and financial success. I got married and have two sons. For the next two decades and more, I spared little time for any spiritual pursuit or even spiritual thought. Consequently, perhaps, when my sons were in their teens, I noticed that they had negligible interest in, or inclination towards, Hinduism. This troubled both me and my wife, as we wondered whether our sons would have a strong enough moral compass if their thinking was not guided by a sound philosophy. We also feared that a lack of respect for Hinduism and ancient Indian thought might dent their sense of self-worth, which in turn might make them defensive in their engagement with the world. This led us to nudging them into doing some minimum prayers every day. However, such conversations always ended quickly, with my sons questioning the logic behind our religious beliefs and practises, and my wife and I having no convincing answers.

It was this inadequacy that made me resolve that until I acquired at least the minimum knowledge required to answer my sons' questions reasonably, I would not broach this topic again with them. I needed first to convince myself that Hinduism was not merely a set of rituals and superstitions.

Thus started a process of reading and assimilating content. Unfortunately, there was no single source that answered all my questions satisfactorily. There was no single material that presented all the key topics of Hinduism in a logical sequence which could help a beginner like me get a basic, yet 360°, introduction to the subject. Therefore, it took me quite a bit of reading, listening and contemplating to find answers to my sons' and my own questions. The clear and unambiguous promise of the Hindu philosophy to deliver unconditional and everlasting happiness ensured that my interest in the subject never ebbed, but only grew, through this whole period of study. And happily for me, the effort was truly worth it. With every passing dose of learning, my hunch turned into a belief, and then into a firm conviction that learning and internalising the key teachings of our philosophy was one of the smartest things my 'success and happiness-seeking' young sons could do.

During this process, I also noticed that almost all Hindu households in my circle were faced with the same issue. The youngsters in these families had little or no interest in the basic Hindu philosophy and were slowly turning into agnostics. In fact, several of these youngsters, in their keenness to be seen as liberals with a 'modern' (read western) outlook on life, were clearly playing down their Hindu roots and identities. It is a pity because given how progressive, modern and empowering Hindu philosophy is, it could hugely benefit our youth in their intensely competitive and challenging lives.

It is against this background that I decided to write a book that could introduce youngsters and beginners to Hindu philosophy. And so here it is - *Hinduism Beneath the Surface - A family's attempt at understanding Sanatana Dharma.* The book attempts to present a structured introduction to Hinduism based on which a person can form a well-informed and considered opinion pertaining to its relevance in his or her life. The book also seeks to provide a broad structure to the vast body of Hindu thought and wisdom, which could help a reader identify areas of interest for further studies. Otherwise, given the vastness of the Shastras, one could feel lost and overwhelmed, and give up even before getting started. And finally, the book attempts to answer some 'Frequently Asked Questions', including some that my sons posed to me when in their teens.

I now welcome you to an introduction to the fascinating world of ancient Hindu thought.

Disclaimer

- This book merely seeks to present an introduction to the Hindu philosophy and does not claim credit for any detailed or in-depth coverage.

- My own progress in this ongoing journey of learning has been minimal, but may well be enough to piece together this introduction.

Chapter 2

Why Should You Read This Book?

Navigating through life's challenges without a working philosophy would be as stressful as trying to solve complex mathematical problems without using mathematical formulas!

Philosophy is a serious subject, and most people find books on the subject rather dry. It is difficult to read a book on philosophy and benefit from it unless one is clear about what one is looking for. Therefore, setting out 'why you should read this book and how you could benefit from it' at the very outset would be in order.

Everything we do can be linked directly or indirectly to either (a) seeking happiness or (b) staying away from suffering. Even between these two objectives, the latter is in fact nothing more than a subset of, or precondition for, the former. In other words, happiness is the sole objective of every person and is the driver of all our thoughts, words and actions. If we pause and recount what we did in the last 24 hours, every single item in that list would link up, either directly or indirectly, to the pursuit of happiness.

The role of any religion or philosophy is to help us in this constant quest for happiness. The philosophy of Hinduism or Sanatana Dharma provides us with a toolkit for happiness. It is almost like a process manual. It first defines what real happiness is, and then goes on to outline a step-by-step process for experiencing real happiness and staying happy.

This aspect of Hindu philosophy is missed by many who fail to see beyond the religious rituals of Hinduism. It is my desire to see more and more young people understand and explore Hindu philosophy, going beyond its religious practises and rituals. It is my firm belief that such an understanding and exploration would uplift our society, particularly our youth. It will empower them in their quest for success and happiness.

Man needs a working philosophy to navigate the challenges of life efficiently. Dealing with life without a working philosophy is akin to solving complex mathematical problems without the knowledge and use of mathematical formulas. Imagine how difficult and stressful that would be!

Life keeps putting us in situations wherein we need to make decisions, choose between alternatives, between right and wrong. And often, we get limited time to make these decisions. We, therefore, need some guiding principles that can help us think and act effectively. This would be particularly true in today's age of relentless information bombardment and opinion shaping by the internet and social media, which leave people with little time for reflection and original thought.

It is in this context that the Hindu philosophy, with its predominant focus on the mind and its management, could prove to be an empowering tool to get the best out of one's mind, and thus one's life. The philosophy helps us base our decisions on correct reasoning, and not just on what is convenient or pleasant. When grounded in reason, we know what we are doing is right. This helps us overcome doubts and also gives us the fortitude to face the consequences of our decisions, even if the outcomes are not always to our liking.

How best to read this book?

The 31 chapters of the book have been organised under seven sections. The sections would give the reader an idea of what to expect in the upcoming chapters and their purpose.

The next chapter introduces a fictional family of four members through an incident in their household. From here on, almost every chapter has two parts:

- The first part (**in standard font**) is largely a compilation of carefully curated points from our scriptural wisdom on the topic.

- The second part (***in italics***) deals with the interpretation of the first part. This is done through conversations on the topic among the members of the fictional family.

Understandably, the first part might seem a little dry to readers, but forms the basis of what follows in the second part. Therefore, a careful reading of the first part of each chapter is key to enjoy and benefit from the second part.

My suggestion to the reader would be to read the first part of each chapter and dwell on it within the mind for a while before moving on to the conversations on the topic. Noting down questions (if any) on each chapter would be useful because the questions that arise in one chapter might get answered in a subsequent chapter that provides a better context for the same. If not, please feel free to email them to me at hbtsbook@gmail.com.

At the end, you may like to check how many of the points in chapter 28 (titled 'Takeaways for the Rajan Family') would sit well as an important takeaway for you and your near and dear ones too.

Chapter 3

A Turmoil in the Rajan Household

A tale not very unfamiliar in several households today!

"Virat says that he does not want to be present for Sunday's puja," Priya said in a tone filled with both shock and pain. "He says he does not believe in our religious rituals and would rather spend the day with his friends. How did we get to this stage, Rajan? Can't we do anything about this? Are we going to just watch our son completely disown our culture, traditions and religion? And what will our relatives say about his absence on Sunday?"

It was a long time since the Rajan household had done any major puja in their home, and this one had been planned a month in advance both as a religious and social event, wherein the wider family would pray together for the welfare of the entire clan.

Virat was twenty-six. After completing schooling at Horizon International School and studying Computer Science Engineering at Bedrock College of Engineering, Virat had been working in a logistics company as a Data Analyst for the last three years. Over the last six months, he had been preparing to move to the US to first pursue a Master's degree and then a career in Data Science and Analytics. Virat had also been dating Neha, his sister's friend, for over a year now. Neha too was working on her plans to pursue further studies in the US. The two had now decided to get married.

Virat's assertion that he would stay away from the event made Rajan angry. He felt his son was being both disrespectful and insensitive. Rajan's immediate instinct was to summon Virat and give him a mouthful. However, better sense prevailed. The last few occasions when they had discussed anything contentious and sensitive had not gone Rajan's way. He, therefore, realised that this matter required a well-considered response based on a deeper understanding of his son's views and the reasons for the same.

The puja was performed satisfactorily but for the incomplete feeling caused by Virat's absence and the discomfort of having to explain it to curious relatives resorting to half-truths and even a few white lies. That very evening Rajan discussed the matter with his daughter Varsha, younger to Virat by two years. An MBA graduate, Varsha was employed in a multinational bank.

"Appa, as we all know, Virat stopped praying after his close friend Raunaq died in a road accident. We had discussed this, and you had remarked then that we should leave him alone and give him some time to heal. However, of late, I get the feeling that Virat has started to dislike Hinduism. I was planning to talk to you and Amma about this. I feel that the social circle in which he spends his time is the reason. He still spends a lot of his leisure time with his college friends."

"Based on my chats with him, most of his friends and professors in his college saw our traditions as totally regressive and full of superstitions. It was not unusual for any student who held a contrarian view to get isolated in his college. That is where the seeds of his views seem to have been sown, and over time things have come to this pass."

"Amma, do you remember the idols of Lord Vishnu that you bought in Tirupati last year, and which you placed on our study tables, one in each of our rooms? Virat has put that idol away somewhere. I no longer see it in his room."

"Virat has now become extremely defensive about being a Hindu. I have heard him announce his lack of belief in our religious practises rather loudly in front of his friends more than once, sometimes quite needlessly."

Both Rajan and Priya found Varsha's words disturbing and worrying. Did they err in the selection of Virat's school and college? How did they completely miss this gradual *shaping of Virat's views? They felt guilty for not having been vigilant and connected enough.*

Post this chat, Rajan suggested that they should address the matter with Virat fair and square, jointly as a family. It was decided that the matter would be discussed the following Sunday. All three also agreed that they would approach this proposed discussion with utmost patience, with a single-minded objective of listening to Virat and understanding him.

When Rajan broached the subject the following Sunday, Virat started off being very defensive and tried his best to cut short the discussion. However, with Rajan, Priya and Varsha steering clear of any confrontation and patiently persisting with their questions that were clearly borne out of genuine concern and love, he started opening up.

"Appa, I do not see how our religion can be of any practical use to me. What problems can it possibly help me solve? For instance, at this stage of my life, I am trying to figure out how to build a successful professional career. By this time next year, I hope to be in the US, a country where you can dream big and also achieve big. How can religion help me in all this? Secondly, Hinduism is so full of superstitions. The pujas and rituals will only complicate my life." Virat appeared to be clear in his mind.

"Virat, you have plans to move to the US. There is nothing wrong with that. However, in my view, you cannot engage confidently with the world if you are defensive about your own roots. It could make you overly eager to

fit in with the Americans in the US. If that happens, you might not receive the respect you deserve. And if with such a mental makeup you choose to settle down in the US for the long term, your children might feel confused about their identity and could even struggle with an identity crisis. It is important therefore that you get informed well enough about Hinduism and form considered views," opined Rajan.

The discussion went on for well over an hour, with Virat doing most of the talking. Virat's perception of Hinduism was shaped by a number of questions for which he was convinced that there could possibly be no acceptable answers. The questions were on the following lines:

- *Why do we have so many Gods?*

- *How can anyone accept this theory of multiple Gods leading human-like lives, marrying amongst themselves, begetting children and even dying?*

- *How can one believe in stories like an elephant's head getting fixed to a human body (as in Lord Ganesha) or a man having ten heads (as in Ravana), and so on and so forth?*

- *Why do we keep chanting shlokas and mantras even when we do not understand their meaning?*

- *Does Hinduism not promote discrimination between people based on the caste they are born into?*

- *Are our Gods corrupt? We offer them a coconut and expect them to grant us our wish in return!*

- *How can Hindu philosophy help in our quest for success and happiness? Is it really relevant to our lives?*

The questions were all perfectly legitimate and merited credible answers. Rajan, Priya and Varsha acknowledged them in no uncertain terms, and this put Virat at ease.

"A few years back, I had read quite a few books on Hinduism and made my own notes under thirty odd headings," began Rajan. "Let me go back to those notes and share them topic by topic with the three of you. Let us discuss and debate each topic. Please trust me on this suggestion and approach it with an open mind."

Rajan's suggestion was not readily agreed to by Virat. "The three of you are positively oriented towards Hinduism, while I am not. I am afraid the discussions could become too stressful for me, and eventually end up as some sort of brainwashing exercise." Virat's fears about getting outnumbered in the discussions were not entirely without basis.

"I promise there will be no attempt to brainwash anyone. I too want a free and fair discussion. After all, if I need to change my current views on any aspect of Hinduism, I would like to understand the same too," Rajan reassured. "And once we are done with these discussions and debates, all of us should respect each other's freedom to form our own views and opinions about religion and spirituality in general, and Hinduism in particular." Virat's fears were allayed somewhat.

Virat eventually agreed to be part of the discussions.

"Let us also agree in advance about the rules for these discussions and debates:

- *We shall approach the discussions with an open mind and try our best to set aside our prejudices.*

- *We shall not see these discussions as some sort of competition among us, which will eventually throw up winners and losers.*

- *We will consciously try not to be cynical or insulting of each other's views. We shall at all times remember and respect that the primary reason why we are having this discussion is that we care for each other.*

- *We will consider each point on its merit - and merit alone. Just because we are unable to accept or agree on a particular point, we will not extend that mood of disagreement to the next point.*

What do you all say?"

Rajan's above suggestions were accepted by the other three in full letter and spirit. The initial unease had by now given way to an understated excitement among all four about the intellectually stimulating discussions that they had all signed up for.

These stimulating discussions happened (in the true letter and spirit!) over thirty-odd sessions. The notes shared by Rajan for each of these sessions, and the discussions that followed, form the content of the rest of this book.

Section B
Fundamental Concepts

This section deals with the fundamental concepts of Sanatana Dharma. Is Hinduism a religion or something more? What is the purpose of our lives as per Hindu philosophy? How does Hinduism define God? What really is this fascinating concept of Maya? Are we merely our body and mind? How does the Karma theory work? If our fate is already predetermined, what is the point of hard work?

A basic understanding of these concepts is essential for one to engage in any discussion or contemplation on Hinduism.

Chapters in this Section

Chapter 4

Hinduism or Sanatana Dharma?

The word Hinduism is a foreign construct. There is no mention of the word 'Hindu' in the ancient 'Hindu' scriptures like the Vedas, the Upanishads, or the Bhagavad Gita. This word is supposedly derived from the word Sindhu, the original Sanskrit name for the river Indus. 'Hindu' was a Persian term used to denote the people who lived in the east, beyond the river Indus.

While the world has coined the word 'Hinduism' and labelled it a religion, are the Hindus merely practitioners of another religion? A study of the core Hindu philosophy clearly shows the answer to be a 'No'. Ancient Indians followed *'Dharma'*. The word *'Dharma'* does not mean religion or faith. It means a 'Way of Life' involving a set of recommendations for how to manage and conduct one's life. This way of life that our ancestors followed is known as Sanatana Dharma or the 'Eternal Way of Life', which, if followed in its true spirit, holds the promise of a happy life and a happy world.

The provisions of Sanatana Dharma are detailed in the ancient Hindu scriptures, of which the Vedas are the oldest. The Vedas are at least 3,400 years old. While this age of the Vedas is a conservative estimate agreed to by Western historians, there are reasons to consider the Vedas to be much older. According to the famous Indian freedom fighter and scholar Bal Gangadhar Tilak, certain astronomical observations in the Vedas show them to be at least 10,000 years old! Therefore, the use of the word Sanatana (meaning 'eternal') might not seem misplaced in the case of Sanatana Dharma, popularly known now as Hinduism.

Given the above, it would perhaps be more appropriate for modern-day Indians, who value their scriptures (Shastras), to call themselves Sanatanis, rather than Hindus. From here on, we will use the words Hinduism and Sanatana Dharma, as well as Hindus and Sanatanis, interchangeably in this book.

The literal meaning of '*Sanatana Dharma*' is 'eternal order' or 'eternal law'. It can also be interpreted as the 'eternal way to live'. Sanatana Dharma delves deep into human life, its ultimate purpose and the ways to achieve this purpose. It helps one to understand oneself better and use that understanding to figure out how one can evolve to one's best state and become the best version of oneself. Based on this understanding, a Sanatani charts his path for achieving life's purpose, such that the pursuit itself fills his life with joy.

Sanatana Dharma helps one to overcome or mitigate **Shadripu** or the six biggest challenges of the human mind, namely, excessive desire or lust (**Kama**), anger (**Krodha**), greed (**Lobha**), obsessive attachment (**Moha**), ego (**Mada**) and jealousy (**Matsarya**), to provide oneself with the best chance of real and sustained happiness.

"It is indeed news to me that the Hindu scriptures do not use the word 'Hindu' at all!" said a surprised Virat.

"It is possible that your current views on Hinduism have been shaped by people who have never bothered to really read and understand our scriptures," Rajan could not resist this somewhat combative quip, though he gathered himself quickly, thanks to a timely nudge on his foot beneath the dining table by Priya.

Fortunately, Virat did not get provoked, as Varsha picked up the conversation **"Appa, what do you mean when you say that Hinduism is, in fact, a way of life and not just another religion?"**

"We should perhaps use the name 'Sanatana Dharma' instead of Hinduism. And Sanatana Dharma, at its core, is nothing but a set of recommendations for leading a purposeful and honourable life. Irrespective of which God you worship, including Gods described in other religions, you could still be a follower of Sanatana Dharma. And that is what I mean when I say that Hinduism is more than a religion. Its messages can find resonance amongst followers of all faiths."

"Are you saying that if I follow the Sanatana way of life, I would qualify as a Sanatani irrespective of the God I worship? For instance, could I be worshipping Jesus and still be a Sanatani?" probed Virat.

"Yes. My understanding is that there is nothing in our scriptures that would seem to prohibit that. In fact, Mahatma Gandhi said 'There is in Hinduism room enough for Jesus, as there is for Mohammad, Zoroaster and Moses.'

'In Sanatana Dharma, the focus is on the way you live and the life purpose that you chase'. For instance, while there was not the slightest element of doubt in *my parents' minds that they were Sanatanis, their puja room had photos of both Buddha and Guru Nanak, along with those of various other Hindu Gods," clarified Rajan.*

"But Appa, Thatha (grandfather) having Guru Nanak's photo in his puja room seems to be an exception and not the rule. Have we ever seen this in any of our relatives' homes? I don't think anyone in our larger family has understood Hinduism this way. These are points that can sound good in a discussion, but I don't see them being practically followed anywhere," said Virat, brushing aside what Rajan had said as a mere theory that is never practised.

"You are digressing," countered Rajan. "The point of discussion is what Sanatana Dharma really offers and recommends, and not how it is being interpreted and practised in general."

"Fair enough. Let me stretch my question a little more. Can I be an atheist and still a Sanatani?"

"Atheism too could be considered a valid philosophical position within Hinduism. In fact, the Charvaka philosophy that rejected the very concept of God co-existed with the Vedic philosophy, even as far back as 150 BCE. It spoke of the world of spirituality and religion as *an aberration. Therefore, it might be fair to say that an atheist or an agnostic too could call himself a Sanatani if he was otherwise following the Sanatana Dharma way of life," said Rajan.*

"Interesting! Can we then go on to the recommendations of Sanatana Dharma?" *asked Virat.*

"Yes, we shall, over the next few weeks through my subsequent notes," said Rajan, concluding the first round of discussions rather peacefully. However, all four members of the household knew within themselves that this was no guarantee of peace in the rounds to come.

Chapter 5

Life's Purpose

The purpose of life according to Sanatana Dharma is to figure out the formula for happiness and always be happy!

As per Sanatana Dharma, the purpose of life is to attain Ananda or Bliss, a default state of **ultimate and perfect happiness**! What is a **default state**? It is the state in which one remains almost always, and to which one returns quickly and automatically, even if pulled out momentarily by external triggers.

Ananda is a state where we are free from all negative emotions like insecurity, fear, hatred, jealousy, ego, anger, or greed. This, in turn, results in freedom from anxieties. Freed from anxieties, we remain more in the present and live life to the fullest. While in Ananda, our hearts are full of joy and love, and we feel both liberated and complete, experiencing a deep sense of peace within. In short, Ananda is the state of the ultimate evolution of a human being.

Ananda is achieved by gaining a deep understanding of the workings of one's mind and its active management based on that understanding. In other words, it is a state of inner happiness that needs nothing else but oneself. However, before attempting to chase and attain Ananda, one needs to understand the difference between Ananda and the generally perceived notions of happiness.

Ananda Versus 'Smaller' And Momentary Pleasures

We often confuse pleasant emotions, triggered by the satisfaction of sense organs or by the acquisition of material possessions, for real happiness. Such pleasures are transitory and not sustainable. Sanatana Dharma warns against the risk of becoming slaves to such pleasures and advises moderation in their pursuit. The obsessive pursuit of these pleasures, to the exclusion of the more important pursuit of Ananda, results in misery in the long run. Even when such pleasure-seeking is satisfied, it generally results in greed for more, only to enslave us and lead us eventually to a state of addiction. And when not satisfied, it culminates in frustration and anger.

Bhagavad Gita (Chapter II, Verses 62, 63)

ध्यायतो विषयान्पुंस: सङ्गस्तेषूपजायते।
सङ्गात्सञ्जायते काम: कामात्क्रोधोऽभिजायते॥

क्रोधाद्भवति सम्मोह: सम्मोहात्स्मृतिविभ्रम:।
स्मृतिभ्रंशाद् बुद्धिनाशो बुद्धिनाशात्प्रणश्यति॥

dhyāyato vishayān puṁsah sangas teshūpajāyate
sangāt sañjāyate kāmah kāmāt krodho 'bhijāyate

krodhād bhavati sammohaḥ sammohāt smṛiti-vibhramaḥ
smṛiti-bhranśhād buddhi-nāśho buddhi-nāśhāt
praṇaśhyati

Translation

"When a man thinks of objects, attachment for them arises; from attachment desire is born; from desire arises anger. From anger comes delusion; from delusion, loss of memory; from loss of memory, the destruction of discrimination; from destruction of discrimination, he perishes." [The Holy Geeta, Commentary by Swami Chinmayananda][1]

Our senses have a tendency to focus outwards. Therefore, by default, we see the outer world, and not our inner selves. We keep getting attracted to external objects, hoping to derive happiness from

---

1 From Swami Chinmayananda's commentary on the Bhagavad Gita, in a book titled "The Holy Geeta"

them. When we keep thinking of any such object in which we perceive happiness, we develop a deep attachment to the same, which leads to obsessive desire. Until the object is attained, it keeps looping in our thoughts. Even if attained, such obsessive desire only gives way to greed for more. If not attained, it leads to frustration and anger, which in turn leads to delusion and selective memory, wherein we remember only whatever justifies our frustration and anger. This results in the loss of the power to discriminate between right and wrong. In such a state, we can commit blunders, which could cause huge destruction, and even be fatal.

Ananda does not lie in external objects of enjoyment, as perceived by our sense organs. It is a state of mind that lies within us. Upon attainment of Ananda, one is not dependent on any other person or thing for one's happiness. Such a person is always in a joyful state, soaking in the bliss within. Worldly pleasures start appearing less significant to such a person.

Let us consider this example:

You may love eating chocolates. However, if happiness is in a bar of chocolate, each successive bar you eat in one go should make your happiness increase proportionately. In other words, if you have ten bars of chocolate in one go, you should become ten times happier. In reality, though, you see the 'law of diminishing returns' playing out. After one or two bars of chocolate, every successive bar gives you less and less happiness, till you can eat no more.

Also, the degree of happiness derived from any specific object or sensory experience varies from person to person. Not everybody likes chocolates equally. What is liked by one may be disliked by another. This proves that happiness does not lie in any object (in this case, chocolate) but within the person. The person's prevailing mood also determines how much he or she can enjoy a particular object. When someone is happy, eating chocolates would be enjoyable. However, it may not be so enjoyable when the same person is in mourning.

Let us now examine what creates this feeling of happiness while eating chocolates. When we bite into a piece of chocolate and start chewing, for some fleeting moments the sense organs are engulfed completely by the pleasant experience of its taste. In this moment, our mind is at peace and free of all thoughts. In this state, in that fleeting moment of 'chocolate happiness', the mind is very close to being silent. It is this quieting of the mind that creates, or results in, the feeling of happiness. In the few moments when the chocolate is in our mouth, our mind is almost rid of all thoughts. As per Sanatana Dharma, Ananda is achieved when one reaches a state wherein one's mind can be kept quiet, at will.

Our scriptures say that it is possible to be in a state free of thoughts, yet fully conscious. This would be a state wherein one is completely in the present. In this context, our scriptures speak of four states of consciousness, namely *Jagrit* (the waking state), *Swapna* (the dreaming state), *Sushupti* (the deep sleep state) and *Turiya* (the 'fourth' state). Amongst these, the first two are states wherein the mind is chaotic and anxious, full of thoughts. The next two (Sushupti and Turiya) are free from thoughts and peaceful.

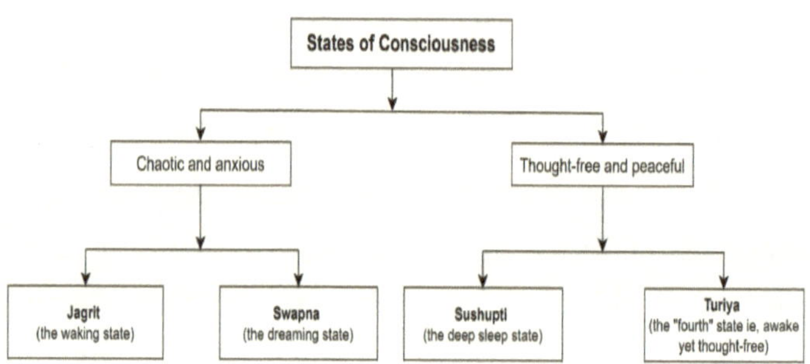

The last state in which one is without thoughts and yet fully conscious in the experience of the present, not thinking of either the past or the future, is a state of ultimate happiness or Ananda. This state is referred to in our scriptures merely as 'the fourth state' (Turiya).

In essence, Sanatana Dharma urges us to turn inwards and to closely observe and manage our minds well. It outlines several processes for us to progressively understand and experience our different planes of consciousness along with their associated happiness, leading us towards the ultimate goal of Ananda.

It was 7 pm on Saturday evening, and it had been raining torrentially, keeping the Rajan family indoors all day. They had bonded over a movie on Netflix and were in a relaxed mood when Rajan initiated the discussions on the note he had shared the previous week.

This time Priya started off. **"I have always known that the purpose of life as per Hinduism is to attain Salvation or Moksha, which is freedom from the cycle of births and deaths. And to attain Moksha, you need to renounce all your desires and reach a state of complete detachment. How can such a completely detached state be a happy or blissful state?"**

"Imagine how terribly boring a state bereft of all desires would be! It sounds so anti-life. Appa, why are you giving this a different twist in your notes?" *Virat was not going to let this one go easily.*

> *"That is what I thought too, until I read more on the Upanishads and the Bhagavad Gita. Moksha is liberation from all anxieties, sufferings and pain, leading to a state of permanent happiness."*

"In fact, the Bhagavad Gita very explicitly says that complete renunciation of a worldly life is not needed to attain Ananda. Our scriptures recognise Dharma (worldly duties), Artha (wealth creation) and Kama (worldly pleasures) as perfectly legitimate aspects of life. It is perfectly fine to pursue these, so long as such a pursuit does not harm any other being, and as long as one does not get addicted to these."

"The Gita cautions one against becoming a slave to these pursuits and prescribes moderation. That said, wealth is not looked down upon in Sanatana Dharma; else we would not have a Goddess of wealth, Lakshmi! Would we?" explained Rajan.

"So this vast and colourful world we see around us cannot offer us real happiness, and it is all within ourselves! Why would anybody accept such a theory?" persisted Virat with his questioning.

"Remember, we are talking of permanent happiness that can never be taken away from us. And since everything in the external world is transient and constantly changing, sustained and permanent happiness can be achieved only by focusing inside ourselves. Isn't that perfectly logical?" countered Rajan.

"And how are we supposed to attain this permanent state of high happiness, which your notes call 'Ananda'?" *asked Varsha in a sceptical tone.*

"Sanatana Dharma does not stop by just outlining the lofty goal of 'Ananda', but goes on to describe a step-by-step process to attain the same. In fact, it provides us with a bouquet of four alternative paths, all leading to Ananda. These are discussed in greater detail in my subsequent notes. At this stage, it would suffice to know that all these four paths involve working on one's mind, understanding it and actively managing it," answered Rajan.

"I liked the chocolate example to illustrate the contention that real happiness is a consequence of a state of mind that is free of thoughts. But then isn't a thought-free state the same as a brain dead state?" *questioned Priya.*

"Not necessarily. Why do we all find deep sleep, which is a thought-free state, so rejuvenating? Don't we all feel very happy and refreshed after a sound sleep?" asked Rajan.

"Even while we are fully awake, any experience that makes us experience high physical or sensory pleasure does so only by fully engulfing our mind within itself. As we saw in the chocolate example, such experiences take us very close to a thought-free state, even if only temporarily.

In all such situations, it is only our proximity to a thought-free state that helps us experience pleasure."

"In fact, our scriptures say that it is possible to be fully conscious in a thought-free state. This is the state of Ananda wherein you are completely in the present. Fully conscious in the experience of the present, not thinking of either the past or the future."

"While such a 'thought-free, yet fully conscious' state is the final level of man's evolution, even slowing down the mind would be relaxing. When we watch a good movie, two or three hours pass very quickly, and we feel happy and refreshed. This is because, for the entire duration of the movie, our mind remains focused on the movie and is not its usual chaotic self with a multitude of random thoughts, fears and worries. In other words, while a fully quiet mind is blissful, even slowing down the mind while still being intellectually alert can be relaxing and refreshing." Rajan's explanation made logical sense.

"But how can the attainment of a permanent state of ultimate happiness be practically possible? It sounds so theoretical and impractical. Why should one embark on this journey of hard work when the end goal sounds so unrealistic and unlikely to ever be reached?" *asked Virat.*

"Firstly, according to our scriptures, it is possible for one at the highest state of human evolution to become

completely immune to all external triggers and remain permanently in Ananda within oneself. Throughout our history, followers of great spiritual masters have seen these great men attain and maintain a state of great peace and equanimity throughout their lives."

"Secondly, since this is a journey that involves working on one's mind continuously to become the best version of oneself, anyone who undertakes it as per Sanatana Dharma can only benefit, irrespective of whether one attains the final destination of Ananda or not. In every stage of this journey, one will find oneself better equipped to handle the challenges and vicissitudes of life, as compared to the previous stage," assured Rajan.

"Would not 'becoming the best version of oneself' in some cases conflict with someone else's happiness, like say in the case of two people trying for the same job?" *asked Varsha.*

"Let us not limit the Sanatana Dharma endeavour to become the best version of oneself to short-term objectives like landing a good job. It is about gaining permanent inner strength, happiness and peace, which would then also manifest as greater ease and efficiency in all of one's dealings with the external world," clarified Rajan.

"How can the same set of recommendations help both a budding tennis player and an aspiring scientist become

their respective best versions? Wouldn't the state of being 'the best version of oneself' differ from person to person? Would that not depend on what one is chasing?" asked Virat.

"*You and Varsha could be pursuing different careers, but ultimately both of you are chasing happiness in your respective lives. Happiness is the common end goal for all of us and is the reason behind all our actions. Becoming the best version of oneself is not the same as merely becoming the best in one's chosen profession. It is about achieving the best possible state within ourselves, which in turn would give us the best chance of experiencing true happiness and remaining happy.*"

"*The Sanatana Dharma promise of unconditional and everlasting inner happiness is relevant to all of us, irrespective of what each one of us is doing in our lives.*"

"*Secondly, if by working on our minds we can reach a high level of alertness and calmness within ourselves, our efforts are bound to be far more effective in all aspects of life. That would give us the best chance of success in all our endeavours, whatever they might be. Additionally, we would remain largely unaffected by adversities and setbacks, and thus gain a much happier state of mind in general,*" clarified Rajan.

"The Bhagavad Gita verse that you have quoted in your notes warns against desire and attachment? I don't like the advice to shun attachment. I would like to remain attached to my near and dear ones, all my life." *Priya clearly was not working with an intent to somehow make her children blindly accept her husband's notes and views.*

"Desire is fine, but not obsession and possessiveness," countered Rajan. "When you keep thinking of an object of desire, it is no longer just desire, but a deep obsession. In this state, even securing the object does not satisfy you. It gives you happiness only for a while before leading to a greed for more. And God forbid, if you do not get the object, you get frustrated and angry, remembering only your pain about not having secured it. In such a state, your actions get taken over by an angry mind instead of a calm intellect. And this could lead to loss and destruction, not only of your material possessions but also your relationships. Have we not seen cases of insecure and possessive parents destroying the married life of their own children?"

"Sanatana Dharma cautions against such obsession and possessiveness, while advocating moderation in desires and attachments. It then goes on further to offer recommendations on how to achieve this balanced state of mind."

"And as for your question about how loving parents can detach themselves from their children, Sanatana

Dharma does not for a minute suggest that you start loving them less. On the other hand, it implores you to expand your love and extend it to others as well, which can ensure that you do not get too possessive about anyone in particular."

"That is easier said than done. These things sound good in theory, but are very difficult to achieve in real-life," *countered Varsha, only to be assured by Rajan that she should wait until she reads all his notes before arriving at any conclusions.*

Chapter 6

God and Godliness

*God is everything and in everything. Godliness is
the intelligence of the universe that scientists have
been trying to figure out forever!*

Sanatana Dharma conceptualises God as the supreme power that is behind the functioning of the universe. While we may be tuned to see only the differences and chaos around us in the world, there are some remarkably predictable things that happen consistently around us (and inside us) all the time, without which our lives would become impossible. If one looks closely, there appears to be some order or intelligence that governs the whole universe, which we take for granted in planning and living our lives.

Let us consider a basic example that we can all relate to, namely the onset and end of different seasons, which is such a fundamental aspect of life on earth. We all know that this happens because the earth orbits the sun. Science tells us that the orbiting of the sun by the earth is due to the gravitational forces between the sun and the earth. But then what is the root cause of gravity itself?

Similarly, we know that without electromagnetism, no life would be possible. Science tells us that it is due to the electromagnetic forces between atomic and subatomic particles that we have different states of matter like solids, liquids and gases. But then what is the root cause of electromagnetism itself? In other words, while science can explain how these properties of nature function, it is unable to satisfactorily explain why these properties happen in the first place and what is their root cause. And when it comes to the functioning of the human mind, human emotions, and the different states of consciousness, these points of consistency and order become even more difficult to explain.

How did this order in the universe come about, and how is it maintained in perpetuity? How does it all work in such a fail-proof manner, with clockwise precision, forever and ever? Our scriptures suggest that there is a bigger universal intelligence at play here. Our own intellect is just a fraction in comparison and is nothing more than a mere tool to try to understand this bigger universal intelligence.

The force behind this all-pervading universal intelligence or order is what Sanatana Dharma refers to as Brahman or God. It describes God as the permanent, highest reality, without which nothing can exist. According to our scriptures:

- God is the cause, the source and the destination for all creation, sustenance, growth and destruction.

- God is in everything. God is the essence in all objects and beings. There is nothing that can exist apart from God.

- God is permanent and unchanging, yet the cause of all changes!

- God is infinite, limitless, and all-powerful.

- God is complete in every way.

- God has all the attributes, and hence, no distinguishing attribute or form. [The Nirguna Brahman (God), beyond any defining form or attribute, is at the core of Hindu philosophy. Having said that, Hinduism also accommodates the concept of a Saguna Brahman. The Saguna Brahman or Personal God with specific forms and clearly described attributes caters to the needs of the common man who needs to worship a form that he can visualise.]

- All that ever has been, is, and can be, is included in God. God can thus also be described as ALL.

- Just like the waves in a vast ocean are mere manifestations of the ocean, so also are all objects and beings mere manifestations in the ocean of ALL [Chandogya Upanishad, VI, ii-I].

- Therefore, God is the ultimate and only truth.

Bhagavad Gita (Chapter VII, Verse 7)

मत्तः परतरं नान्यत्किञ्चिदस्ति धनञ्जय।
मयि सर्वमिदं प्रोतं सूत्रे मणिगणा इव॥

mattaḥ parataraṁ nānyat kiñchid asti dhanañjaya
mayi sarvam idaṁ protaṁ sūtre maṇi-gaṇā iva

Translation

"There is nothing whatsoever higher than Me, O Dhanañjaya. All this is strung in Me, as clusters of gems on a string" [The Holy Geeta, Commentary by Swami Chinmayananda][2]

Here, God's omnipresence has been described using the example of a necklace. In a closely strung pearl necklace, we cannot see the string between any two pearls. Nor can we see the string running through

---

2 From Swami Chinmayananda's commentary on the Bhagavad Gita, in a book titled "The Holy Geeta"

each pearl. Yet we have no doubt about the existence of the string within and without every pearl in the necklace.

Rajan and his family were driving to Mysore to attend the engagement ceremony of his nephew. En route, the family had stopped near Srirangapatna for a sumptuous breakfast of Idli, Vada, Masala Dosa and coffee. The mood in the car was happy when Rajan steered the conversation towards this note.

"This definition of God as the reason for the universal order, which provides the degree of predictability so essential for life, is interesting," *started Virat on a contemplative note.*

"However, if God is beyond attributes and forms, why do we worship idols and photos?" *Varsha seemed to be in a mood to debate.*

"The formless God cannot be visualised, experienced, and meditated upon by most people, but only by the truly evolved. Though we know that God is formless, human beings always seek someone to whom they can pour out their minds and draw solace and peace from. The idols and photos fulfil this human need," clarified Rajan.

"But surely we do not need so many forms. Why do we worship so many Gods like Shiva, Vishnu, Ganesha and so many more? Is that not contradictory to your note which seems to speak of a single God or Brahman who pervades everything?" *Varsha's questioning was perfectly legitimate.*

"For this, you need to understand the unique Hindu concept of Ishta devata or Personal God, which, according to me, is one of the most amazing conceptions by man. According to Sanatana Dharma, one of the ways of achieving life's purpose of Ananda is through Bhakti Yoga or the path of love. In Bhakti Yoga, you expand your love from 'me and my family' to envelop the whole world. The concept of a Personal God aids this process. By presenting God in numerous, fantastic forms, our sages have ensured that each one of us would definitely find at least one form very appealing. As a consequence, most Hindus develop a special bond with their Personal God right from their childhood. If, by your innate nature (Prakriti), you are a man of action and a go-getter, you might like Krishna. If you are extremely conscientious with a great sense of duty, you might like Rama. And if you are a believer in experiences and living in the moment, you might like Shiva."

"And once you have identified your Personal God, developing love or Bhakti for that Personal God, and nurturing and growing that love becomes relatively

easier. The wonderful stories glorifying each of these forms that our sages have left behind ensure that you remain a fan for life."

"Sometimes the choice of a Personal God gets aligned with a profession and the common challenges encountered in that field. For instance, wrestlers and bodybuilders generally tend to pray to Hanuman, while construction workers pray to Vishwakarma, and so on. The stories of these Personal Gods inspire the devotees to face their unique challenges more efficiently to achieve their professional goals."

"But how can we believe in such totally unrealistic concepts like a God with a human body but an elephant's head, or a king with ten heads, or a child God who lifts an entire hill with his little finger, or a monkey God who flies carrying a mountain in his hands?" *Virat was in no mood to pull his punches.*

"These fantastic stories are the surest way to effortlessly initiate even children into understanding, and eventually exploring, the concepts of God, religion and spirituality in a progressive manner."

"As a concept, this is not very different from the love for characters like Spiderman, Batman and Superman that we find today even amongst adults. Even though these characters and their stories are so unreal, people

watch their movies again and again. That is because they have been in love with these characters right from their childhood. Similarly, many of us fell in love with the stories of Krishna, Hanuman and Ganesha in our childhood and retain our love for them even as adults.

"That said, the core Hindu philosophy is very clear about the one, absolute, formless God. The Kena Upanishad asserts, not once but five times in five verses, that reality is your own Self within you and not what you worship here in this world.

"On another subject, our mythological works involving these various forms of Gods also carry great moral lessons for children to imbibe easily." Rajan's explanation was both comprehensive and effective.

Chapter 7

Maya or Ignorance

The world you see is not the complete truth!

As per Sanatana Dharma, none of us, other than those who have attained the ultimate state of Ananda, can perceive (see, hear, smell, taste, or feel) every single thing that is present around us with a hundred percent accuracy. This is because we are engulfed by Maya or ignorance. Hardly anybody is seeing everything that is present or happening all around them, or even right under their nose. There are many reasons for Maya:

- We cannot be at multiple places at the same time, nor can we travel in time. The five senses by which we perceive our world, and on the basis of which we form our opinions, are severely limited. For instance, we can hear sounds only within a certain frequency range, and there are colours our eyes cannot see. Our perceptions exclude far more than what they include. Maya is therefore inevitable.

- Everything in this world is dependent and interdependent, subjective and relative. People's perceptions, in particular, are entirely subjective. People do not bear in mind the fact that everything is constantly changing, and that nothing is permanent. This results in their opinions and conclusions generally falling short of the truth.

- People's views on others are based on whatever they know about those others. However, every person has a long life story, most of which no one else can possibly know. This lack of knowledge shrouds us in Maya, because of which we often arrive at wrong conclusions and opinions about others.

- Likewise, a person's station in life also determines how he perceives the world. A young father might see his children as vulnerable and needing protection, while in his old age he might see the same children as his guardians.

- Also, the same person could be perceived differently by different people at the same time. A young man would be a father to his son, a child to his father, and a loving husband to his wife.

- Generally, we see and hear only what our mind, shrouded in Maya, lets us see and hear. Maya functions in the form of our ego, emotions, desires, likes, dislikes, etc., which are nothing but where our Prakriti (innate nature shaped by the sum total of our experiences) has led us to.

Notwithstanding the above, it is difficult for people to accept that whatever they actually see around them is not the real truth. That said, wouldn't we all agree with what Swami Chinmayananda says in his book Kindle Life, "Mirage can never be true. And even when we 'see' the mirage, the desert alone is the reality in it!"[3]

The only way to overcome Maya is through real knowledge and awareness. A man could mistake a rope in a dimly lit room for a snake and experience intense fear. The rope is the truth, while the snake is Maya. Not recognising the rope is the root cause of mistaking it for a snake. This illusion-led fear of the snake can never be removed except by gaining the knowledge that it is, in fact, a rope. Therefore, Maya can only be eliminated by real knowledge.

The degree of Maya that a person is limited by depends on how far a person is from reaching a state of full evolution or Ananda. Blinded by Maya, most people spend their entire lives chasing material things in the

---

3   From Swami Chinmayananda's book 'Kindle Life'

external world, wrongly perceiving happiness in those things. Such a relentless pursuit of material possessions and sensory pleasures, to the exclusion of the pursuit of inner Ananda, is bound to result in progressively more negative emotions like greed, insecurity, fear, hatred, jealousy, ego and anger, drowning the person deeper in misery. In a completely realised state, i.e. the state of Ananda, one's perceptions are no longer impaired by Maya.

Within a day of Rajan circulating this note, Virat himself initiated the discussion over dinner. **"If we interpret this concept of Maya literally and start treating everything around us as unreal, how can we live in a society and transact with the world?"**

Rajan smiled, sensing that his son was beginning to enjoy these discussions.

"I agree. Some of our Sanskrit shlokas sound so categorical in dismissing the whole material world around us as an absolute myth. That is difficult to digest," *added Priya.*

"You cannot just look at the literal translation of any single shloka or verse, without taking into account the context in which it appears. The world around us is not a myth. It is the way we see and understand the

world that is flawed. Our views and opinions have severe limitations due to the narrow lens through which we see the world. Further, everything in the world is transient and constantly changing. However, we do not adequately factor this into our thoughts and actions. We cater to our emotions and obsessions, often without applying adequate thought. We chase material achievements and acquisitions as though they can give us permanent happiness, only to realise later that the happiness is short-lived. We get excessively possessive about things and people as though they are going to be with us forever, only to suffer when they are no longer with us. This happens again and again, but still we persist with this approach to life and keep hurting ourselves," said Rajan.

"We see what our eyes fall on. What then do you mean when you say that we only see what our mind lets us see?" *asked Varsha.*

"Let us consider a performance by a celebrity sportsman in a sporting event. His die-hard fan would talk about only the good aspects of his performance, while his critic would only speak about his shortcomings and mistakes. Neither of them is deliberately trying to mislead. It is just that they have only seen what their mind allowed them to, and missed what their likes, dislikes and prejudices did not let them see. However, a neutral person who is

neither a fan nor a critic might be able to objectively assess the sportsman's performance since his degree of Maya in this instance would be lesser."

"In other words, your truth is always different from my truth, and both are always different from and lesser than the real and full truth. That is why our scriptures say that this whole world that we see around ourselves is shrouded in Maya." Rajan's example of differing views on the same performance of a celebrity sportsman was quite effective.

"You say that Maya can only be fully removed in our ultimate state of evolution or Ananda. Till then, how are we to deal with and respond to what we see and perceive all the time?" *Priya was looking for practical suggestions.*

"What we see, touch and feel might not represent the full truth, but is certainly part of the truth. The gap is in the way we perceive and interpret these experiences which results in Maya. Maya then distorts our responses, leading to suffering."

"As we progress in our journey of awareness about ourselves and the universe, the quality of our perceptions and responses also keeps improving, getting more and more effective at every stage."

"Even in our current state, we can use the above understanding of Maya to realise and accept that no

matter how hard we try, our independent perceptions and views about anything are subject to serious limitations. Reality is always more than what we can see, feel and perceive. This realisation should make us better listeners to other points of view, and also more observant. Once we internalise this, our differences with others will come down, as well as our frustrations caused by such differences.

"Secondly, the concept of Maya can also help us to understand that emotions are the outcomes of mere perceptions and are seldom based on the full truth. That is why emotions are subject to change and could also go away with time. A carefully cultivated state of constant awareness about Maya will help us to distance ourselves from extreme emotions and always approach the issues at hand with a calm mind."

Rajan's answers provided good food for thought for the other three as they retired for the day.

Chapter 8

Who am I?

We are much more than our body and mind!

Are we our body? Or are we our mind? Is there something more to us beyond these two? According to our scriptures, we are neither our body nor our mind. Our true identity or real self is our soul, i.e., **Atman**.

Atman is a speck of God inside us. It is our direct connection with the divine. It provides the spark of life or the life energy to our body, which otherwise is inert matter. We attain a state of Ananda when we experience and identify ourselves with our Atman. However, it is difficult to experience our Atman because it is veiled from our perceptions by *Shareera Traya* (our three bodies) spread over *Pancha Koshas* (five sheaths or layers). These are explained below.

The *Atman* stops after providing the life energy and does not interfere in our actions. It is a mere witness to all our actions, always remaining in a state of complete peace, harmony and bliss. Atman is deathless or immortal. It is continuously seeking a total merger with *Paramatma* (God) and is constantly moving towards that goal. In death, it is only our body that dies, while the Atman enters a new body to continue its onward journey towards Paramatma. The merger of our Atman with the Paramatma is inevitable and could happen within one lifetime or take many lives, depending upon our Karma.

To work towards this merger with the Paramatma, resulting in Ananda, is the purpose of our lives. It happens when we transcend the Pancha Koshas or five sheaths, to perceive and identify ourselves with our Atman. This is a state of full peace and love, wherein we feel complete and one with the entire universe. There are no fears, cravings, or sufferings in this state. It is the perfect state, i.e., the fully 'merged with God' state, or *Ananda*.

As stated above, the Atman is veiled from our perceptions by Shareera Traya (our three bodies) spread over Pancha Koshas (five sheaths or layers). Let us examine all these different terms and concepts briefly. The **Annamaya Kosha** or the food sheath is our body that takes birth and perishes. This is the most gross aspect of our existence. We can take care of our body by eating the right food and being regular in some form of exercise. The Annanmaya Kosha is also known as our **Sthula Shareera** or gross body. However, we are not just our body. Beyond the Sthula Shareera, we also have a subtle body or **Sukshma Shareera**.

The Sukshma Shareera extends over three sheaths, namely the Pranamaya Kosha, the Manomaya Kosha and the Vijnanamaya Kosha, as explained below. The **Pranamaya Kosha** is the sheath of our vital life energies. Upon birth, breathing starts only after a brief delay. That is why Prana is more than mere breath. It can be described as the sum total of our vital life energies that drive all our internal bodily functions. A uniform flow of Prana to each and every cell of the body keeps the body alive, functioning and healthy. We can nourish our Pranamaya Kosha through Pranayama.

The **Manomaya Kosha** or the mind sheath is a conglomeration of thoughts. The mind keeps changing and fluctuating, sometimes happy, sometimes unhappy. The mind houses the emotions, which are nothing but thoughts in a loop, often driven by ego. It is characterised by feelings such as love, hate, likes and dislikes. When such emotions become powerful, they start controlling and directing our actions, often against what is right. That is why Sanatana Dharma places a huge emphasis on the management of the mind. Even modern medical science acknowledges the huge impact of the mind's functioning on our health. We can nourish our mind or the *Manomaya Kosha* by following the dos and don'ts prescribed in the *Vedas* (*Yamas* and *Niayamas*, as detailed under the topic Raja Yoga), culturing our emotions (as detailed under the topic Bhakti Yoga), pursuing and gaining true knowledge (as detailed under the topic Jnana Yoga), or by engaging in selfless service (as detailed under the topic Karma Yoga), all of which could help us transcend the typical failings of the mind.

Then comes the **Vijnanamaya Kosha**, or the intellect sheath. As per Sanatana Dharma, the intellect is distinct from the mind. It is the intellect that defines our ability to discriminate between good and bad, or right and wrong. This is the layer that differentiates humans from animals. We can nourish this layer by acquiring more knowledge and wisdom, and through meditation. The following quotes from Swami Chinmayananda's book *Kindle Life* bring out this difference between the mind and intellect more clearly.

- "The mind is an instrument of feelings and emotions while the intellect is the one which discriminates and judges."

- "The functions of the mind and intellect are fundamentally divergent and opposed to each other. For example, when a person is overwhelmed with emotions, his faculty of discrimination is lost, and when acute discrimination prevails, there is no room for sentiments and feelings."

- "There is no one who is the purely intellect type or the purely mind type." (which means that everybody is a mix of both; only the proportion varies from person to person)

- "The secret of success behind all men of achievement lies in their ability to apply their intellect in all their activities without being misled by any surging emotions or feelings."[4]

We now come to the fifth sheath or the **Anandamaya Kosha**, which is the equanimity or bliss layer. It has the closest proximity to our true self, the Atman. It therefore enjoys the reflection of the blissfulness of the Atman, which is a place of stillness, peace and deep inner joy. We experience Anandamaya Kosha during deep sleep, which is a state of thought-free and trouble-free rest. It is a state when the experience of the other four sheaths is blanked out. These other sheaths are all there during deep sleep but do not manifest. When we wake up from deep sleep, we feel refreshed and rejuvenated.

---

4   From Swami Chinmayananda's book 'Kindle Life'

And if we do not get deep sleep, we miss it, which means we do experience it. As our **Karana Shareera** or our causal body, the Anandamaya Kosha is the most subtle of the five sheaths. According to Sanatana Dharma, in deep meditation, an evolved seeker can let go of the Anandamaya Kosha too. When this most subtle layer is thus transcended, we reach the Atman, our very essence. This is the perfect state, i.e., the fully 'merged with God' state, or Ananda.

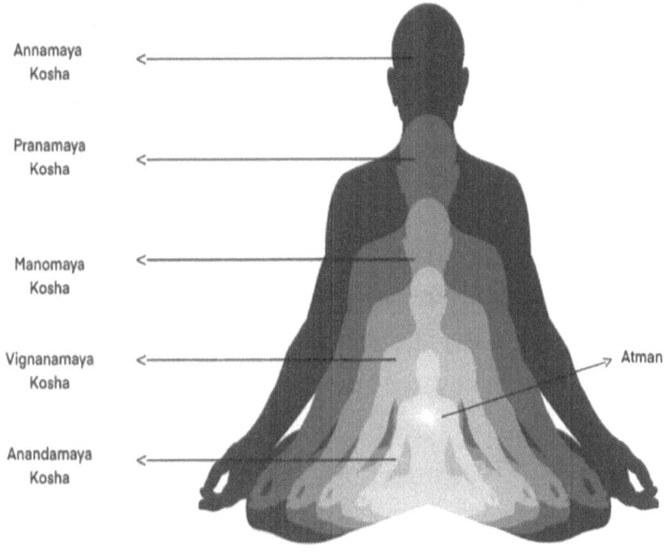

The five sheaths spread across our three bodies can be mapped as follows:

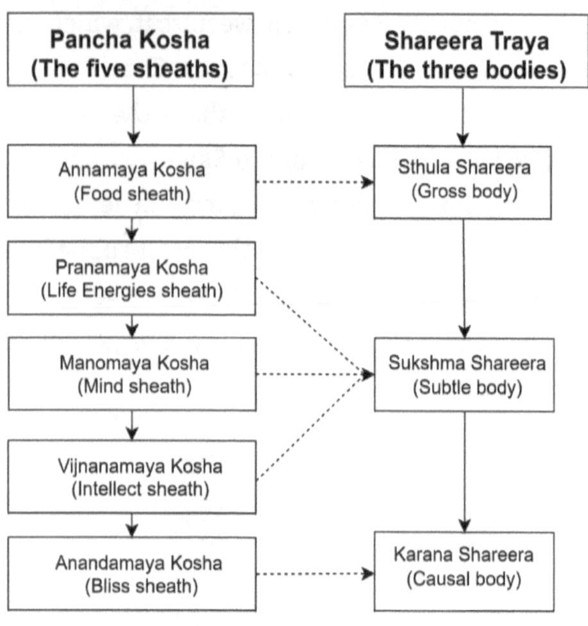

To illustrate this concept of Atman (our real self) covered by the Koshas, Katha Upanishad uses an example of a passenger being driven by a charioteer in a chariot (pulled by five horses) towards his destination. If we correlate this to our journey of life, the passenger represents the Atman, the chariot our body, the charioteer our intellect, the reins our mind, and the five horses our five senses i.e., sight, hearing, smell, taste and touch. Our sense organs (the horses) pull our mind in different directions, constantly distracted by external objects in which they wrongly perceive happiness. In such a situation, it is only our intellect (the charioteer) which can keep us on the right path by managing the mind (the reins) to control the senses (horses) and take us to our destination (Ananda).

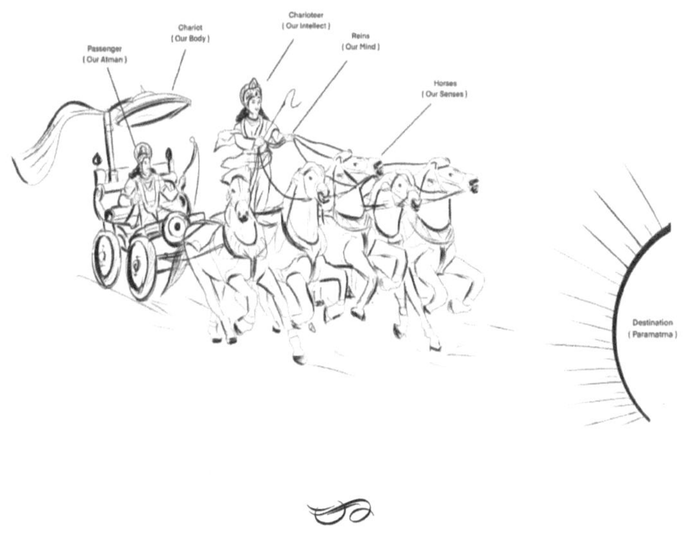

"This gets a little too fuzzy, Appa. It is very difficult to imagine myself as separate from my body." *Varsha was spontaneous in her expression the moment the discussions started around Rajan's note.*

The family had come out post-dinner to a neighbourhood ice cream shop to celebrate Varsha's promotion to the position of a manager in her job. It was 10.30 pm, and there was nobody else in the shop other than the four of them. As usual, the ice creams were delicious and facilitated an energetic and happy chat.

"Even if we accept that we are distinct from our body and mind, the concept of our intellect being a separate entity from our mind is not very convincing," added Virat.

"And the concept of Anandamaya Kosha, or a bliss layer, is quite a stretch of imagination." Priya was clearly not sold on the concept of Pancha Kosha.

"I believe the concept of Pancha Kosha is easier to understand intellectually, but difficult to experience fully. There is an interesting conversation between a son and his father, a wise sage, detailed in Bhrigu Valli of Taittiriya Upanishad. I will use my own adaptation of that conversation to explain the concept of Pancha Kosha." Clearly, this was one of Rajan's favourite topics.

"Varsha, we are clearly much more than our body. Else, there would be no difference between a man and a dead body!"

"OK, we breathe. A dead body does not. That makes us body plus breath," reacted Varsha spontaneously, shooting from her hip.

"There you go. Your breath is a part of the second layer, the Pranamaya Kosha. So we have accounted for two of the five sheaths, namely, the Annamaya Kosha and the Pranamaya Kosha."

"However, it does not stop there. We are definitely more than our body plus Prana. Else, what would be the *difference between you and a person who is in a coma, totally brain dead?"*

"Fair enough. I can think and feel different emotions, while a brain dead person cannot. That makes us our body plus prana plus mind." *Virat's tone was more curious now.*

"Yes, the mind that houses our emotions is the third sheath, the Manomaya Kosha. However, it does not stop there. Take the case of our neighbour, Suresh. He is older than you but is always so emotional. He gets easily provoked and gets into major fights frequently. He has resigned from three jobs within a span of eight months. Clearly, his uncontrolled emotions are messing up his life and career."

"And now compare Suresh with Arun, my colleague's son. Though he is Suresh's batchmate, he seems distinctly smarter in his career decisions. Right? Now, what does Arun have that Suresh does not? The ability to control his emotions, and discriminate better between right and wrong. That ability comes from better use of the fourth sheath, the Vijnanamaya Kosha or our intellect. As against the mind that is capable of only emotions, the intellect helps us discriminate between right and wrong in any given situation."

"Waiting to see how you explain the fifth sheath or the Anandamaya Kosha." *Priya was curious.*

"You mean the bliss sheath. We experience it every day during deep, dreamless sleep. It is a state when our body, mind and intellect are completely blanked out. Despite this, we still experience the state. We feel so refreshed after a deep sleep and miss it when we are deprived of it."

"In a waking state, the closest we can get to Anandamaya Kosha is perhaps as a small joyful baby, when we have no accumulation or baggage in our minds. The baby's experience of life is pure, unadulterated by thoughts. The baby lives fully in the present, totally free from troubles like regrets of the past or worries about the future. That is why we often see small babies laughing and smiling joyfully for no apparent reason."

"Some gurus believe that we experience Anandamaya Kosha when in a state of flow, doing what we love, where we lose sense of time, completely absorbed in what we are engaged in. You may find that at times great sportspersons get into a different zone altogether, wherein they look immune to external pressure and pull off incredible performances. The same with great musicians. At times, they get so immersed in their own music that the rest of the world ceases to exist for them. That is when they produce their best music, providing *an unreal and magical experience to their audience. It happens even to us at times. Sometimes we get completely into something that we enjoy. It could be our work. We get into a zone wherein the difference between the experience and the experiencer vanishes, just for the duration of that experience. That is when we are close to Anandamaya Kosha."*

"Likewise, there is yet another view that says that when you are either the recipient or giver of true love, the inner happiness you experience is because you get close to this bliss sheath."

"Hmm... what about another round of ice creams?" *Varsha was keen not to allow the discussion to completely take over the celebration of her personal success. "Yes" was the unanimous response.*

"What then is the difference between this fifth layer and our Atman? Both have been described as pure bliss in your notes," *Virat resumed the conversation as the family settled down with their second serving of ice creams.*

"The examples of Anandamaya Kosha that we discussed speak of rare instances wherein we experience Ananda. However, when the experience of such Ananda becomes our default state, we can say we have identified ourselves with our Atman, the real us," explained Rajan.

"Is Atman and Soul the same?" *asked Varsha.*

"Yes and No. If in other religions an individual is seen as a body with a soul, the Hindu scriptures see an individual as a 'soul' (Atman) that is temporarily residing in a body, which it will discard at the end of each life, only to be born again in a new body with a new life. This cycle of births and deaths goes on till Atman attains its purpose of realisation of Ananda through a merger with Paramatma or God," said Rajan.

"Have you ever seen, or even heard of, anyone who lived in the last 100 years and who attained the ultimate state of Ananda?" *asked Virat.*

"Not really. Obviously in such a state, you cannot have even a trace of ego or negativity in you. There cannot be any anger towards anyone. If I go by these yardsticks, I find some of the famous modern-day gurus falling short. However, if I go by what my trusted elders have told me, the late Ramana Maharishi seemed to have attained that state during his lifetime.

"We should also remember that once someone reaches that plane of existence, they would have gone beyond all need to exhibit that state to the world. So we may never easily come to know about such people."

It was 11.10 pm, 10 minutes past the scheduled closing time of the ice cream shop. The staff at the shop seemed to be waiting impatiently for the family to finish eating their ice creams and leave. As the family left the shop, Rajan tipped the young man behind the counter. All in all, it had been a happy evening for the Rajans.

Chapter 9

The Karma Theory

At its most elementary level, the Karma theory is not very different from the concept of 'as you sow, so you reap'. Every deliberate act through one's body, mind or intellect is Karma. In other words, every thought, word or action is Karma. Every Karma, whether good or bad, has an associated impact which manifests as an experience for the person who performed the Karma. Every deliberate action triggers a reaction that has to be necessarily experienced by the person who performed the action, either in this birth or in a future birth.

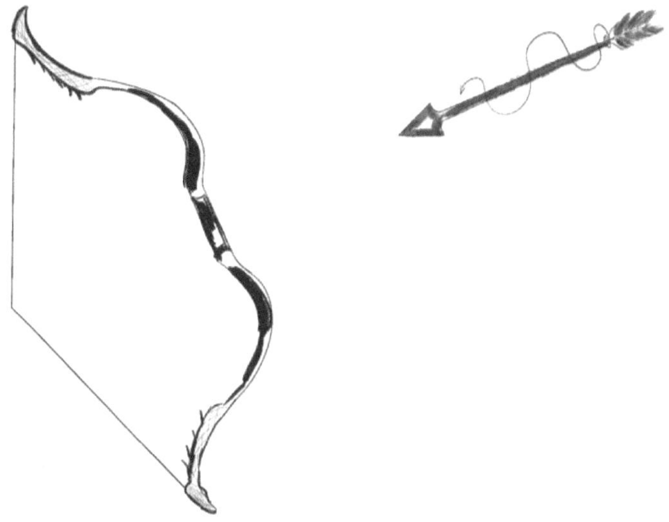

While one can exercise control over one's Karma, one has no control over the timing or extent of the reaction. The reactions do not follow the sequence of the original Karma. It could happen in any sequence. It may happen in this lifetime or the next, or after several lives. Many of the pleasant and unpleasant circumstances we encounter are the result of our Karma in our previous births. At the time of our birth, we come with the seed of several challenges and opportunities already implanted in our life.

Types of Karma

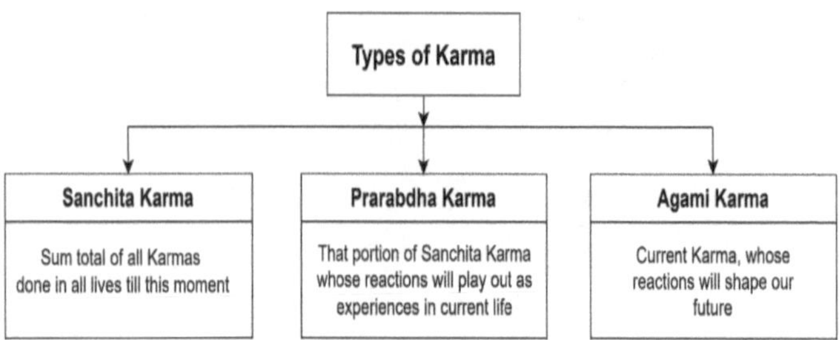

- **Sanchita Karma** - This is the vast accumulation of all our previous Karma including that from our past lives, which is yet to manifest as reactions. One cannot change this. Its reactions have to necessarily play out, in this life or in future lives. Sanchita Karma could take several lives to manifest fully.

- **Prarabdha Karma** - A portion of our Sanchita Karma from past lives also accompanies us to play out its reactions in each life. Prarabdha is that portion of our Sanchita Karma that is responsible for the circumstances that we face in our present life. When the reaction to a past Karma manifests now as an experience, we can attribute it to Prarabdha Karma. In other words, whatever we are going through in life presently on which we have no control is our Prarabdha Karma. It cannot be prevented but can only be exhausted through experience. Let us say we are swimming across a river to reach the other side. The flow of the river's current and its direction as we swim, rendering the swim either easy or difficult, is the result of our Prarabdha Karma.

- **Agami Karma** - Agami Karma is our current Karma, the choices we make right now and the deliberate actions we perform as a result of those choices. We will experience the reactions to Agami Karma in the future, either in this birth or a future birth.

As stated earlier, the impact of every Karma manifests as experiences, and to experience anything we need a body and mind. That is why we keep taking births after 'every' death, till we have exhausted the impact of all our Karma by experiencing their reactions. The path that the Atman takes after the death of one's body is determined by our Karma and our unfulfilled desires at the time of death. Each new birth happens in a body and in a setting that is most suited for the person to realise his unfulfilled desires from the previous birth and also to experience the impact of Prarabdha Karma that is earmarked for the new life.

As we evolve through the right Karma, we start moving beyond the grosser layers of our existence like the body and mind and move closer to the subtle layers. In the process, we shed our constricted egoistic personality and start identifying ourselves more and more with the whole universe. Our actions gradually cease to be driven by petty and selfish interests. We merely do what has to be done in every situation. None of our actions are driven by ego or a feeling of 'I-ness'. In other words, we no longer act with a feeling of doership, i.e., 'I am doing'. **No Karma sticks to us anymore.** Eventually, we experience and identify ourselves with our core essence or our Atman. When there are no further manifestations of past Karma left to be experienced, we get freed from the cycle of life and death.

It had been two days since the government had imposed a three-week-long nationwide lockdown to arrest the spread of COVID. With no option to step outside the house, the four members of the Rajan household were getting a lot more time together. And to everybody's surprise, it was turning out to be much more fun than what they thought it would be. This also allowed for more frequent discussions on Rajan's notes.

"If what we get in life is entirely determined by our Karma, why do people pray to God? Can God be persuaded to change the way the Karma theory shall apply in our lives?" *Virat's tone sounded sarcastic.*

> *"Prayers cannot change the adverse circumstances you might be plunged into because of your past actions. However, prayers can infuse hope and confidence in people and help them navigate those circumstances better," said Rajan.*

"Does this mean that our entire life is already predetermined, and that nothing is in our control?" *asked Varsha.*

"Absolutely not. Our free will and personal efforts are supreme," said Rajan. "Let us discuss that part after I share my next set of notes, titled 'Fate versus Free will'."

"The Karma theory is based entirely on the premise of rebirth. Is there any credible evidence of rebirth?" *asked Virat.*

"While there is no irrefutable proof of rebirth, there are some documented cases that suggest that its possibility cannot be dismissed outright. Worldwide, there have been numerous instances of children who reported that they have memories of a previous life. I read somewhere that more than 2,500 cases have been studied and their specifications published and preserved in the archives of the Division of Perceptual Studies at the University of Virginia (United States) alone."[5]

"People who believe in rebirth put forward the following arguments:

- *How can children of the same parents growing up in the same environment be so different in their physical, intellectual and emotional makeups?*

---

5   https://med.virginia.edu/perceptual-studies/wp-content/uploads/sites/360/2015/11/REI35.pdf

- *What explains the countless instances of child prodigies, where even infants have displayed unreal levels of skills in areas that require decades of practice?*

- *How do some children display such clear likes and dislikes from a very young age, not reconcilable with their life experiences?*

- *What explains the cases of extremely competent people unable to achieve what they are chasing in life, while people with low competencies seem to achieve those very goals with ease?"*

"Look at Anisha and Shweta," Rajan was referring to his niece's children. "They are twins, yet to reach teenage. This means that they have had minimum influence from the outside world. They are growing up at the same time, in the same house, interacting and learning from the same set of people. They are going to the same school. Yet how come they are so different in their innate nature. Anisha is so organised, while Shweta is quite the opposite, yet very talented."

"Even if I assume that we indeed go through multiple births, I fail to understand why the reactions to our Karma spill over to another birth. Would it not have been better if the results fructified in the same birth? Would that not have ensured the total wiping out of bad Karma

from this world?" *Priya's question stemmed from her desire to see a world free of sin and suffering.*

"Such a system of Karma and its full reaction within the same birth would completely nullify the importance of free will. Since the intent behind the Karma is more important than the Karma itself, only deliberate actions done out of free will can be termed as Karma. Where a Karma is driven by the carrot of guaranteed rewards, or abstained from under the threat of definite retribution, the role of free will gets severely diluted. Under such a rule, most humans would react to any given situation in a similar way. Real intent will stop determining actions." Clearly, Rajan had gone through this several times in his mind.

"Don't you think that concepts like rebirth are mere distractions? I can't see how belief in the Karma theory can help us in our lives?" *Varsha's question was perfectly legitimate.*

"Irrespective of whether we accept the concept of rebirth or not, we can definitely use several aspects of the Karma theory to better our lives. The broad Karma theory principle of 'as you sow, so you reap' does inspire us to think and act right."

"Ups and downs will be inevitable in every life. The Karma theory tells us that our difficulties are our own doing and the

result of our own past Karma. This helps us accept and own up to the 'downs', instead of remaining in denial or sulking at our bad fate. Furthermore, several great commentators on the Karma theory have said that between fate and free will, the latter will always be supreme. This is elaborated in my next set of notes titled 'Fate versus Free will'. This inspires us to work hard to overcome the challenges that life throws at us, rather than sulking about our fate."

"Lastly, by stating that our true Self or the Atman is eternal, the Karma theory also helps us to overcome the fear of death and the related anxieties, and to always remain positive and optimistic," said Rajan.

Virat smiled to himself, wondering how his father managed to give a positive twist to all aspects of the Sanatana Dharma philosophy.

"Right now some common Karma seems to be affecting all Indians and making them experience this lockdown," commented Varsha with her tongue firmly in her cheek.

"The lockdown might be common, but its experience would be entirely different from person to person," quipped Priya, having the last word.

Chapter 10

Fate (Prarabdha) Versus Free Will (Purushartha)

You can fight your fate and win!

Fate, by definition, is invariable and binding. That is why it is called Prarabdha or destiny. On the other hand, free will is independent, variable and, by definition, free. That is why it is called Purushartha or personal effort, that we are free to determine and shape. That brings us to the question of what is more important, Prarabdha or Purushartha, Fate or Free Will? Should the Karma theory be interpreted to mean that everything that is going to happen in our lives is already decided by our **Prarabdha** (previous Karma)? If so, are our personal efforts or **Purushartha** just a waste of time and energy?

"Certainly not," says Sri Chandrasekhara Bharati Swaminah, the Late Shankaracharya of Sringeri Sharada Peetham, in a book titled *Dialogues with the Guru* which presents a series of talks with the Shankaracharya, compiled by Shri R Krishnaswami Iyer. The following points (a to d below) are inspired and adapted from the above book.

a. **Our Free Will shapes our Fate**: Fate is the result of how we have exercised our free will up to this point, across previous lives as well as in the current one. If we apply this logic to the future, our present exercise of free-will should shape what lies ahead. In other words, just as our current circumstances are the result of our past choices, our future can be moulded by our present actions, over which we have significant control.

b. **Fate is a signal of the efforts required**: We should have faith in the power of free will and commit wholeheartedly to it. By exercising our free will wisely and acting accordingly, we can shape both our present and our future. Whenever we encounter a high resistance to our efforts, instead of seeing it as an obstacle put up by our fate, we should see it as fate's signal about the level of effort needed to achieve our goals.

c. **Keep scaling up your efforts till your challenges are overcome**: We typically anticipate the effort required for any task based on our understanding and past experiences. However, if such efforts prove insufficient to achieve the desired results, we should treat it as a signal that our past exercise of free will may have been inappropriate. Therefore, we must scale up our current efforts suitably to address the same. Seeing the hurdles we face as a consequence of our own past actions also provides us with the confidence that if we had the capability in the past to create these hurdles, it should be within our ability now to eliminate them.

d. Let us consider an example of a nail driven into a wooden pillar that we need to pull out. We may see just a small portion of the nail projecting out of the pillar. The rest is embedded inside the wood, and we cannot see how long that is. Neither do we know the strength and composition of the wood. Can we say how much effort will be required to pull out the nail? The length that is inside is not arbitrary, but is the result of the number and intensity of strokes that drove in the nail in the first place. This represents the way we have exercised our free will in the past. If this nail must be pulled out, we do not stop pulling merely because we do not know how deep it has been driven into the wood. We keep trying, using different tools, till the nail comes out fully. We need to approach every effort of ours with the same mindset. Try as hard as you can, including upskilling yourselves suitably as may be required, with the conviction that you will succeed eventually.

There's no point in sulking over comparisons of our fate with that of others, or in complaining that someone less talented achieved more success with lesser efforts. If success is about being in the right place at the right time, it is Karma that determines who lands up in those right places at the right time. If success eludes us initially, we must keep striving through the right Karma to get into those advantageous positions in the future.

Our horoscope could at best be a picture of the probable implications of our past on our future, as indicated at the time of our birth. It is not a precise account of how our life will pan out because it does not take into account the free will led Karma that we have already done in the present life since our birth or will do in the future. Swami Chinmayananda in his book Kindle Life says "'What' one meets in life is destiny and 'How' one meets it is self-effort.....The future, therefore, is a continuity of the past modified in the present"[6]

6   From Swami Chinmayananda's book 'Kindle Life'

In this context, it is also important to understand the Hindu concept of **Shakti**. In our scriptures, the energy that drives all acts of creation, sustenance and destruction is referred to as Shakti. Without Shakti, all of existence is simply lifeless matter. Hindus worship this divine energy or Shakti through feminine forms like Goddess Parvati, Goddess Durga and Goddess Kali.

It is Shakti that helps us in steering our efforts from **Sankalpa** (resolve) to **Siddhi** (achievement of objectives). There are three types of Shakti representing the three key requirements for achieving success in any human endeavour:

- Iccha **Shakti**: The power of desire leading to firm resolve or **Sankalpa** is the first step.

- Jnana **Shakti**: The power to equip oneself with the requisite knowledge and skills (Jnana) to perform the action is the second step.

- Kriya **Shakti**: The power to apply that knowledge and skill to bring one's resolve (Sankalpa) to fruition or **Siddhi** is the third step.

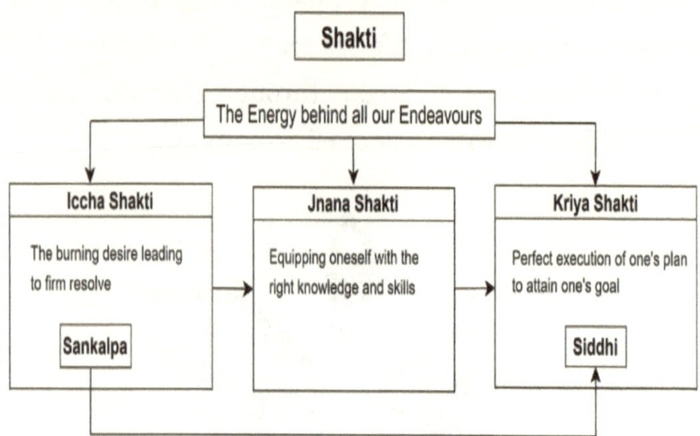

The above three elements of firm resolve, 'planning and preparation', and effective execution are key for success in any major human endeavour.

From the above, it is clear that there is no place for despondency and inaction in Sanatana Dharma. The solutions to adverse challenges in life lie only in our efforts, backed by courage, determination, and perseverance.

"The concept of Iccha Shakti, Jnana Shakti and Kriya Shakti is very interesting. To see these three factors

separately as three distinct prerequisites for success in any endeavour is indeed useful," said Priya.

"Yes, it is. It teaches us that unless you want something badly, your resolve to do it is never firm enough. In other words, without adequate Iccha Shakti, there can be no Sankalpa or firm resolve. It then tells us that firm resolve may by itself not be good enough to overcome tough challenges. It has to be supported by Jnana Shakti or necessary preparations in terms of learning and skilling yourself for the task undertaken. And finally, after all the preparations, if you do not have the Kriya Shakti or the ability to put everything into action, your efforts would come to nought, and you cannot attain Siddhi or success in your endeavours."

"Appa, when my friend Raunaq died in that road accident, a really promising life was cut short so cruelly by fate. How could he have avoided that with his free will? And his parents are such kind people. What could they have possibly done to deserve such unimaginable pain?" Virat's comments showed the profound impact which Raunaq's untimely death had on him.

"I understand your pain, Virat. When I was your age, I lost my sister under extremely unfortunate circumstances. We have spoken about this once. She was an absolute angel. All of us in our family were totally devastated. We felt neither she, nor any of us, deserved a fate like that, not even remotely. It made no sense, and for a long time, there was no closure.

"If we go by our scriptures, the only possible reason for what Raunaq and his parents went through is Prarabdha Karma from past lives, manifesting in this birth as experience. It is impossible to figure out now whether Raunaq could have done anything differently to avoid the accident or mitigate its impact. As for his parents, they need to focus their free will now on picking up the pieces, strengthening themselves within and making the rest of their lives as purposeful and happy as possible.

"In my personal view, it is only the Karma theory that provides a somewhat palatable explanation for events that seem so utterly and grossly unfair."

Rajan's comments led to a contemplative silence for a few minutes.

"I find the concept of fate a little depressing. The challenges I face in life are the result of what I did in the past or in my previous births, none of which I can undo now. Would this not breed a feeling of helplessness?" Varsha's question was filled with anxiety.

"The challenges you face today may not be in your control, but you do have control over what you are *going to do now to overcome those challenges. Therefore, instead of sulking over why you are faced with challenges, start fighting those challenges by putting your best foot forward."*

"Secondly, not all your past Karma would manifest only as tough challenges. They could also manifest as doses of good luck! Why assume all your previous actions were bad? Aren't you happy to be part of the top 1% of candidates who applied to IIM in your batch and successfully gained admission?" Rajan's answer made Varsha smile.

Section C
The Suggested Paths

This section deals with the 'how do I get there' aspect, after the previous sections have defined the purpose of life. It deals with the different paths suggested by Sanatana Dharma with respect to attaining and retaining the state of ultimate happiness, and some related concepts.

This section is akin to a process manual, with Do's and Don'ts and real-life examples.

Chapters in this Section

Chapter 11

Your Prakriti and Gunas Decide your Best Path

Your innate nature makes you do things that might look extremely stupid in hindsight!

Sanatana Dharma does not stop merely by showing us a lofty goal of vanquishing Maya and attaining Ananda. It provides us with a toolkit to achieve the same, consisting of four possible paths for us to choose from, namely, **Karma Yoga**, **Jnana Yoga**, **Bhakti Yoga**, and **Raja Yoga**. All the four paths are tools that help us shed our ego and the feeling of 'I-ness'. Rid of selfishness, we get freed from greed, jealousy, frustration, stress and anger. This results in deep inner peace, and eventually in Ananda.

The four paths are not mutually exclusive. **To navigate our journey towards Ananda purposefully,**

most of us might need to incorporate elements of all the four paths in our lives, with one of them becoming the primary and dominant driver of our evolution. One should choose this dominant driver based on a careful understanding of one's innate nature or **Prakriti**. A person's Prakriti is shaped by his past actions and experiences through all lives, both current and previous.

According to our scriptures, one's Prakriti manifests through one's Gunas or qualities. Gunas are of three types - Tamas, Rajas, and Sattva. Every human being has all three Gunas. However, the proportion and degree vary from person to person, and it is this proportion that determines the person's Prakriti. Let us now examine the three types of Gunas that make up our Prakriti.

Tamas means darkness. Tamas is characterised by resistance to action, in the form of laziness, drowsiness, and sleep at a physical level, and resistance to thinking and analysing at a mental level. A Tamasic person lacks ambition, initiative and energy. His key attribute is dullness. Eating and sleeping are his favourite activities. Tamas makes a person avoid facing the problems of life, thus limiting his growth. Such a person is often indecisive and cannot discriminate between right and wrong. He is often reckless and delusional. A completely Tamasic person understands neither himself nor others around him and therefore fails in all his relationships.

Rajas means passion. A Rajasic person is dynamic and an active go-getter, with great skills in planning and execution. However, the actions of such a person are driven primarily by the desire or greed for name, fame, money, personal achievement and ego fulfilment. Ego is strong in Rajas, leading inevitably to tensions and stress. A Rajasic person can even adopt immoral and cruel ways to achieve his goals. Having said that, big achievements and great societal good can also come out of such a person's activities.

Sattva means goodness or purity. The defining characteristics of a Sattvic person are purity of heart and intentions, honesty and compassion. A Sattvic person is free from ego, insecurity, selfishness, greed, jealousy, anger and hate. Such a person is enthusiastic yet equanimous in all situations. Balance is a defining feature of a Sattvic person. However, a purely Sattvic person might struggle at times to be decisive when caught between duty and ethics. He could get numbed into inaction in such situations. An example would be Arjuna's predicament in the battlefield of Mahabharata, where he finds himself unable to fight the war, caught in confusion between right and wrong.

It is a person's Prakriti that generally drives their Karma and how they respond to a particular situation. In Chapter III, verse 33 of the Bhagavad Gita, Lord Krishna says:

"सदृशं चेष्टते स्वस्या: प्रकृतेर्ज्ञानवानपि|
प्रकृतिं यान्ति भूतानि निग्रह: किं करिष्यति||"

sadṛiśham cheṣhṭate svasyāḥ prakṛiter jñānavān api
prakṛitim yānti bhūtāni nigrahaḥ kim kariṣhyati

Translation

"Even a wise man acts in accordance with his own nature; beings will follow their own nature; what can restraint do?" [The Holy Geeta, Commentary by Swami Chinmayananda][7]

People's actions are generally determined by their Prakriti or innate nature. To rise above one's Prakriti is not easy, even when one's intellect realises the need to do so in a particular situation.

Therefore, if one wishes to improve one's Karma, one needs to understand and work on one's Prakriti. For doing so, one should first assess one's predominant Guna (Tamas, Rajas or Sattva) dispassionately. One should then strive to move up the 'Guna' ladder step-by-step, by moving the Tamasic aspects of one's nature to Rajas, and the Rajasic aspects to Sattva.

---

7   From Swami Chinmayananda's commentary on the Bhagavad Gita, in a book titled "The Holy Geeta"

When one transcends the three Gunas and thus one's Prakriti, one is said to have become a **Gunatita**. In a Gunatita state, man's intellect is always in control, and he adopts the Guna that is most appropriate for the occasion. A Gunatita does not get emotionally disturbed, is equanimous in both happiness and misery, in the pleasant and the unpleasant, in honour and ignominy. Such a person's dealings are driven only by the demands of the situation. He acts most appropriately even in the most adverse and challenging times, fully retaining both the sensitivity and sharpness of his faculties. Unattached action is the hallmark of a Gunatita. One can be a Gunatita only in a highly evolved state. Krishna in Mahabharata is an example of a Gunatita.

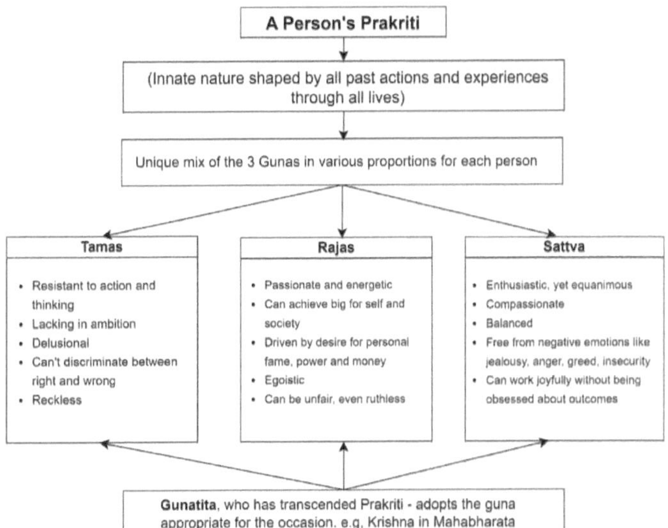

The government-imposed COVID lockdown was still on, and the Rajan family was enjoying a cup of tea on their balcony.

"Appa, I feel you have been predominantly Rajasic. The way you have been chasing personal growth and money in your career does not have anything Sattvic about it. Also, your anxiety relating to the outcomes of your efforts shows on you often." *Virat was being brutally honest.*

"Being Rajasic is better than being predominantly Tamasic though. Not waking up until twelve noon every Sunday, or putting off important work for a later time regularly would qualify as Tamasic, right?" *quipped Varsha, springing to her father's defence spontaneously.*

"Look who's talking. What about not organising one's wardrobe shelves for over a year?" *asked Priya, as she joined the other three with a plate of pakoras to go with the tea.*

> *"Most adults are predominantly Rajasic, Tamasic to a lesser extent, and Sattvic to an even lesser extent," said Rajan, going on to add, "that is no justification though for not striving for more of Sattva."*

"But then if your innate nature or Prakriti is formed by millions of experiences through hundreds of lives, how can one possibly change it?" *Virat's question had a slightly* *sarcastic tone and seemed to be more about the Sanatana concept of multiple lives rather than Prakriti.*

"That is the primary challenge in our lives. Our Prakriti will always drive our mind to react instinctively in most situations. However, if our intellect is alert enough, it can step in just in time to figure out if such an action is right or wrong. According to our scriptures, developing such an alert intellect is the key to attaining Ananda."

"That sounds easier said than done." *Varsha clearly sounded sceptical.*

"Difficult, but not impossible. This is dealt with in greater detail in a subsequent set of notes, which deals with the overall aspect of mind management. Let us discuss this after we have read those notes," suggested Rajan, while adding, "However, please try and ascertain your predominant Guna to figure out which of the four Yogas would work best for you as your primary path to Ananda. We will ask this of each other after we have discussed the four Yogas in some detail," suggested Rajan.

"That would be fun," *said Virat, reaching for the pakoras.*

"Yes. We will also know how honest you are in your self-assessment," *quipped Varsha, as she beat Virat to the last piece of pakora on the plate.*

Chapter 12

Duties Are Not Negotiable Though

You owe a debt to the world that you must repay!

Irrespective of which path one adopts in the pursuit of Ananda (be it Karma Yoga, Bhakti Yoga, Jnana Yoga or Raja Yoga), doing one's duties diligently is of utmost importance, as per Sanatana Dharma. Our Shastras have elaborated upon our duties. First and foremost are the duties towards the family, i.e., parents, spouse and children. Then comes the guru, followed by the poor and weak, guests, and even enemies. Then there are duties as a responsible citizen of any society or community to which one may belong, and duties towards one's nation. And finally, the duties towards every living and non-living being in this world.

Below are key duties, elaborated with some quotes from our scriptures:

Duties Towards Parents And Gurus

- Our parents deserve the utmost respect.

- Our gurus (teachers) too need to be always honoured. The Upanishads ask us to treat both our parents and gurus as Gods.

Duties Towards One's Spouse

- A husband and wife are one and the same.

- The South Indian sage Sayana of the early 14th century says in his commentary on Rig Veda, 'the husband and wife, being the equal halves of a single entity, are equal in all aspects; both should cooperate and participate equally in all work, whether religious or secular'.

- A husband should be loving, protective, sheltering, and tender.

- A wife should be loving, sweet and devoted.

- Mutual fidelity should continue until death.

Duties Of A Parent Towards Children

- It is the duty of every parent to fulfil the needs and wants of children in terms of food, education, clothing and shelter.

- The parent should inculcate the right values in children.

- The parent should be the protector of children during their childhood.

- The parent should also ensure peace at home for the healthy growth and development of children.

Duties towards others, particularly the poor, weak and needy

- It is one's duty to help the underprivileged. One's true happiness lies in becoming a channel through which the grace of God can flow to the weak and needy.

- One should not expect gratitude for the service that one renders to others. The service should be selfless.

- As Swami Vivekananda said, "Love the poor, the miserable, the downtrodden and the Lord will bless you. Never vaunt of your gifts to the poor or expect their gratitude, but rather be grateful to them for giving you the occasion of practising charity to them. Be grateful that the poor man is there, so that by making a gift to him you are able to help yourself. It is not the receiver that is blessed, but it is the giver."

Duties Towards Women

- Women must be honoured and adorned by male members in every family.

- Where women are dishonoured, no ritual or rites can yield any fruit.

- Where the women live in grief, the family soon perishes utterly; but that family in which they are happy, prospers forever.

Duties Towards A Guest

- The Upanishads say, "Atithi Devo Bhava," meaning a guest is akin to God.

- Guests should always be honoured, fed and entertained.

- No guest should ever be turned away.

Duties Towards An Enemy

- One should help even an enemy when the enemy seeks help or forgiveness with humility. Forgiveness is purity; the world is upheld by forgiveness.

- If even an enemy comes to one's home, one should receive him in such a way that he will forget that his host is an enemy (Srimad Bhagavatam 8.16.6).

"Varsha, Sunita aunty is eager for her son Rohan and you to meet each other. I have met Rohan. He is a charming, good-looking young man and runs a successful startup. Would it be all right if I share your phone number with Sunita?" asked Priya, hoping to encourage Varsha to consider the opportunity.

"Amma, I have told you so many times but you just do not give up. Let me repeat yet again. Don't push me towards an arranged marriage. I do not need your or Appa's help to find a partner for myself just yet. If I ever feel the need, I shall not hesitate to seek your help," said Varsha in an irritated tone.

"It is not merely a help. It is also my duty as a parent to do whatever I can to ensure your happiness," explained Priya.

"The way you interpret your duties towards me is scary, to say the least. It does not stop with just supporting and guiding me until I reach adulthood. It has now extended to trying to find a good match for me, and will perhaps extend in the future to helping me even in the parenting of my children. If these are the standard duties of parents, I would rather not marry, let alone have children!" Varsha said, her irritation clear.

"I don't think there is any need to stretch things so far," countered an equally agitated Priya.

After an uncomfortable pause of a couple of minutes, Varsha said **"In reality, what you are trying to do is to pressure me into an arranged marriage, in the guise of doing your duties."**

"Merely suggesting that you meet someone, whom I feel might turn out to be a good match for you, does not amount to pressuring you into an arranged marriage. You can consider the proposal just as you would consider any other potential partner that you might come across," said Priya.

"Alright, let us pause this topic and talk about something else," said Rajan, clearly concerned that the conversation may soon escalate into an emotional and angry exchange.

"Incidentally, the conversation has set up the context for a chat on your Sanatana Dharma note on duties," said Virat with a smile, trying to lighten the mood in the room.

"The duties listed in your notes would be quite a challenge for anyone." *This was Varsha, grabbing the opportunity to shift quickly away from the previous discussion.*

"Duties towards an enemy! Do you believe that common people would have acquitted themselves well against such a list, even in those ancient Vedic times?" *wondered Virat, knowing fully well that nobody in the room was likely to have an accurate answer to that question.*

"I see some inequality in the suggested duties towards the spouse. Why is the word 'devotion to spouse' used only for the wife, and not for the husband? Why do our scriptures seem to demand a greater degree of commitment from a woman as compared to a man?" *asked Varsha, championing the cause of women's rights. Virat nodded in agreement.*

> *"You need to view these suggested duties in the context of the times they were written in, and how society might have been at that time. Even in a country as developed as the USA, women won their right to vote only in 1920, even though the country gained independence from its colonial masters in 1776. And here we are quoting from scriptures that are 3,000 to 4,000 years old," countered Rajan.*

"Don't you feel that prescribing duties in such detail could impinge on personal liberties?" *Virat's 21st-century mind was understandably leaning towards rights, as opposed to duties.*

> *"As compared to the world's current focus on rights, the Sanatana scriptures seem to attach much higher*

importance to duties. The underlying thought seems to be that the performance of duties and responsibilities by everyone in society would automatically secure everyone's rights."

"Another key reason for this high emphasis on duties was also to ensure that no one embarked on a personal spiritual journey of abstinence and meditation, abandoning his responsibilities to family and society," clarified Rajan, emphasising the fact that duties can never be abandoned in the name of spiritual pursuits.

"Given the emphasis on different roles for men and women, does that not need to change in today's world? How can something that has been articulated in such detail and followed for centuries be changed or evolved?" *asked Varsha.*

"If you look carefully, that change has already happened substantially. Roles of people within society and rules for societal engagement will evolve continuously to suit prevailing realities, and that is inevitable. However, the core messages of Sanatana Dharma like the agent of real and lasting happiness being inside us (and not outside), the importance of working on our minds, the techniques prescribed for mind management, and the need to imbibe the values of non-violence and tolerance are truly timeless," said Rajan.

Chapter 13

Karma Yoga - Path of Selfless and Joyful Actions

Working selflessly for a good cause, free from the pressure of outcomes, can yield great happiness and peace!

If you are full of energy and are driven by a passion to make the world a better place, Karma Yoga could be the path most suited for you. A Karmayogi never tries to escape or withdraw from the world. He is continuously engaged with the world.

The key aspects of Karma Yoga are

- **Engaging in action joyfully without ego or a sense of 'I am doing' or 'doership'.** For example, a Karmayogi who is involved in rendering service to the needy never feels that he is serving someone else. He merely feels like a channel through which the divine energy or grace is passing to the receiver of the service.

♦ **Being detached from the outcome of action.** A Karmayogi sets tall goals because goals are important to provide direction and motivation. He then plans in detail, pursues and executes his plans with maximum efficiency, enjoying every moment of the goal chase. However, he does not burden himself with fears and anxieties about outcomes. In other words, in Karma Yoga **having Goals is fine, but not being obsessive about outcomes.**

This aspect of detachment from the outcomes of one's actions is best summed up in the popular verse (No. 47 from Chapter II) of the Bhagavad Gita that says:

कर्मण्येवाधिकारस्ते मा फलेषु कदाचन ।
मा कर्मफलहेतुर्भूर्मा ते सङ्गोऽस्त्वकर्मणि ॥

karmaṇy-evādhikāras te mā phaleṣhu kadāchana
mā karma-phala-hetur bhūr mā te saṅgo stvakarmaṇi

Translation

"The right is to work only, but never to its fruits; let not the fruit of action be thy motive, nor let thy attachment be to inaction." [The Holy Geeta, Commentary by Swami Chinmayananda][8]

According to our scriptures, man's rights are limited to doing actions, but not to any outcome that he may seek through such actions. After all, the results of our actions are dependent not only on our efforts but also on a host of other factors like our past karma, the efforts of others, and the past karma of others. Therefore, we should focus only on our efforts and not get anxious about outcomes. Excessive fears and anxiety about the outcome of any action will not only impair our efficiency with respect to the action but also rob us of enjoyment in doing the action.

A Karmayogi engages in his work joyfully. The work itself is the source of joy for him. He suffers from no anxiety about the results of his work. These two aspects are interrelated. If we remain too anxious about outcomes, the process of working cannot be a source of joy for us. How far we embrace the quality of 'unattached action' would also determine the degree of joy that we can derive from the action.

There is another aspect to making work itself a source of joy. For this, the work that is best suited to one's

---

8   From Swami Chinmayananda's commentary on the Bhagavad Gita, in a book titled "The Holy Geeta"

Prakriti and strengths should be preferred over other work. Chapter III, verse 35 of the Bhagavad Gita says:

श्रेयान्स्वधर्मो विगुण: परधर्मात्स्वनुष्ठितात्।
स्वधर्मे निधनं श्रेय: परधर्मो भयावह:॥

shreyān swa-dharmo viguṇaḥ para-dharmāt
sv-anuṣhṭhitāt
swa-dharme nidhanaṁ śhreyaḥ para-dharmo
bhayāvahaḥ

Translation

"Better one's own duty, though devoid of merit, than the duty of another well discharged. Better is death in one's own duty. The duty of another is fraught with fear." [The Holy Geeta, Commentary by Swami Chinmayananda]

It is better to be our natural selves than try to be someone else. Work suited most to our Prakriti and our inherent strengths is what we will do easily and enjoy the most. We may get attracted to what someone else is doing, but if that is not aligned with our Prakriti, it will cause stress, disturb our peace, and hinder our spiritual evolution.

Perhaps it is most appropriate to speak of ego in the context of Karma Yoga. Ego can become a major obstacle to rendering selfless service without a feeling of 'I am doing', and without worrying about outcomes. Some points about ego:

- Of all the negative attributes that a man can possibly have, our scriptures are most critical of ego. Ego could be defined as one's identity in one's own mind that is based on an excessively high opinion of oneself, leading to undue importance to oneself in all thoughts, words and actions. A highly egoistic person wallows in excess pride, annoys and angers others often, and feels wronged, hurt and angry very easily.

- Ego severely limits our intellect and colours our views. None of our views or judgements about the world can be accurate unless we eliminate ego or reduce it to negligible levels.

- One has to be alert to prevent ego from stealthily creeping into one's psyche. 'Sakshi Bhava' or witnessing the mind (detailed in a subsequent chapter) is a good technique to fight ego. Using this technique, one can become a constant witness to one's own responses and reactions in one's interactions with the world. Such constant alertness can pre-empt ego from entering our mind and help us to take charge of our words and actions.

- Once the ego is overcome, we realise that in reality we are not distinct from anyone else in this universe. We start feeling one with the entire universe, leaving no room for anger, jealousy, fear or hate.

- With the ego vanquished, the fear of failure disappears. And with no fear of failure, work becomes joyful.

- An 'ego-free' person's engagement with the world is more harmonious and less stressful. They can carry people with them easily, and therefore achieve much more. They live in lasting happiness and peace.

From the above, it is clear that shedding our ego is the key to doing Karma without a feeling of 'I am doing'. Until we achieve this state, irrespective of how noble our work, we can consider ourselves only a **Karmi**, and not a **Karmayogi**. A Karmi's actions attach to him and therefore he has to experience their results, both good and bad, through one or more lives. On the other hand, a Karmayogi who performs all his actions without any feeling of 'I am doing' gains immunity from their outcomes and reactions.

In essence, therefore, we strive to make all of our actions pure and selfless in Karma Yoga. When we achieve that, we move closer to God and eventually become one with God.

How do we ascertain whether a particular action is good or bad? The following could serve as some general guidelines:

- **The motive behind the Karma is more important than the Karma itself.** By itself, no action is either good or bad. An action should be deemed as good if the intent behind that action is good. In other words, an action becomes noble or otherwise based on what it strives to achieve.

- Let one not do anything to others that one doesn't wish to be done to oneself.

- Let one wish for others all the good that one wishes for oneself.

- To promote union is to promote harmony. Does the proposed action promote union or separateness? If union, the action is right. If separateness, the action is wrong.

- Any action that calms the mind is right. Conversely, anything that disturbs the mind is wrong.

- To give joy to others is right. To give pain to others is wrong.

* 'Harmlessness' (not harming others) is the highest *Dharma* (duty). We should not injure anyone.

* A man's speech should cause no annoyance. It should be both truthful and beneficial.

* According to Paramahamsa Yogananda, an ideal man is one who is "softer than the flower, where kindness is concerned; stronger than the thunder, where principles are at stake."

The above are general guidelines and may not hold true in all situations. Morality is relative. It is also related to prevailing circumstances. The sin of not killing one who deserves to be killed is the same as the sin of killing a person who should not be killed. A soldier cannot practise non-violence in a battlefield.

In summary

* Karma Yoga involves surrendering oneself to a cause for which one works tirelessly and selflessly without a feeling of doership.

* In Karma Yoga, one finds joy in doing the work itself, without worrying about the outcome of that work.

* The path of Karma Yoga is most suited to those who are pursuing ambitious plans to better the fortunes of their society, nation, or the entire world.

Happily, in Karma Yoga, there are many unfoldments in the journey. The benefits are felt at each step, making the journey itself joyful.

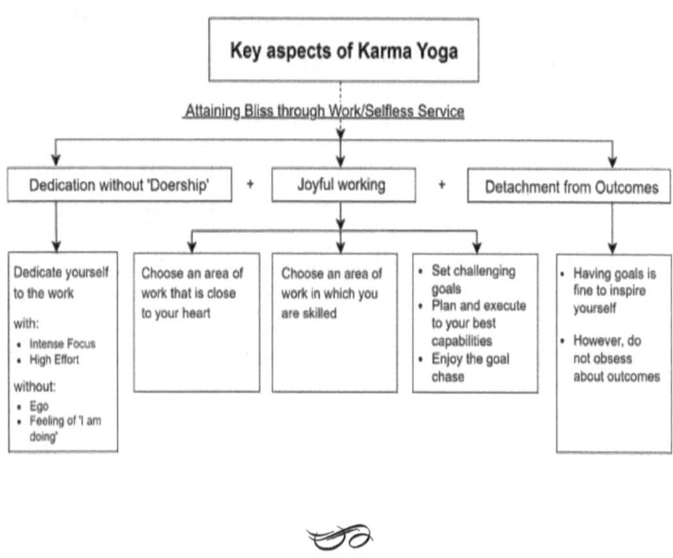

The Rajans were in the lobby of Right Cure Hospital. Rajan's younger brother's wife, Sujata, had developed sudden pain in her abdomen and had to be rushed to the hospital. Her husband was abroad on a business trip. The doctors had recommended an immediate appendix surgery. The surgery was underway. The doctors had assured that there was nothing serious and that Sujata would be fine soon. The initial tension had given way to some relief, and all four members of the Rajan family were in a relaxed frame of mind, waiting in the hospital for the surgery to be completed.

Rajan had shared his note on Karma Yoga just two days ago. After a while, the four started discussing the note as they waited in the hospital lobby.

"Does a Karmayogi have to be a believer in God? This does not appear to be a prerequisite in your notes," asked Priya.

"To a Karmayogi who dedicates his life to a noble cause, the cause itself becomes akin to God or Godliness. Such a person may not feel the need for any religious or spiritual practice. There is no bar, though. People who embark on a path of Karma Yoga may also worship various forms of God or engage in meditation for deriving the strength to remain steadfast in their path even when faced with grave obstacles," clarified Rajan.

"Appa, I hope you would not get upset if I say this. While we are all proud that you have set up a charitable trust that works for the welfare of the underprivileged, I felt that you were flaunting it with a sense of 'I am doing this', while speaking about it to Amma's cousin the other day. You were clearly showing off and appeared to be massaging your own ego." Varsha chuckled as she made her point, making both Priya and Virat burst out in laughter.

"You are right. I have caught myself doing that on a few occasions," said Rajan with a slightly embarrassed smile, while adding, "that is clearly a part of my Prakriti which is dominated by Rajas Guna. This is something that I need to overcome. I need to overcome this 'I am doing' feeling and start seeing myself more as a channel through which divine grace is flowing to its rightful recipients. I am determined to be more watchful in the future, using my Sakshi Bhava."

"That said, you should also realise that the success of my trust depends on the support it receives from others. So I have to necessarily speak about it to more and more people. But from now onwards, I shall remember to be more humble whenever I do so," assured Rajan.

"The path of Karma Yoga seems very interesting indeed. But then, how does one know whether one is suited to such a path, and whether it would work?" queried Virat in all earnestness.

"Identifying a goal that resonates with one's heart and aligns with one's skill sets is the key to success in Karma Yoga. Working on such a goal can itself become a source of joy, irrespective of outcomes," explained Rajan.

"You will find Karmayogis in all walks of life, be it sports, music or films. Such people always appear to be enjoying their work because their interests and skills both align in their work. Even in politics, you would see some leaders work tirelessly and selflessly for *decades to create the world they want to see. They are least affected by electoral losses and appear immune to relentless criticisms by their opponents. They are able to do so because, apart from being skilled in their field, they are also committed to an ideology that is close to their heart. So if you take to Karma Yoga and are keen to remain committed to that path, choose your area of work wisely. That would be half the job done," added Rajan.*

"Can you name some people we all know who could qualify as a Karmayogi?" *Varsha's tone seemed to suggest that she had already thought of some names.*

"I view Nelson Mandela as a true Karmayogi. In his relentless fight to free South Africa from racial discrimination, he endured decades of imprisonment and oppression. Despite his immense suffering, he harboured no hatred. After guiding his country to independence from brutal colonial rule, he forgave his former captors, showing that his struggle was never driven by personal animosity," said Priya.

"Sardar Patel was also a true 'Karma Yogi'. He dedicated his entire life to liberating India from colonial rule and then to uniting and strengthening the nation. Even though he was reportedly the favoured leader among many in the Congress party to be its president

and consequently India's first Prime Minister, he was selfless in accepting Mahatma Gandhi's preference for Jawaharlal Nehru to lead the nation," added Rajan.

Nelson Mandela   *Sardar Vallabhbhai Patel*

"These are such famous people, often described as 'once-in-a-century' personalities. Can a common man even aspire to be a Karmayogi in his lifetime? Have you seen and interacted with anyone who you feel is a Karmayogi or at least has the potential to evolve into a Karmayogi?" *asked Varsha, looking at Rajan.*

"Talking about people who have the potential to be a Karmayogi, I must say I was extremely impressed by Rohan, the person Amma suggested you meet," responded Virat. "We have common friends and have met about half a dozen times, and on each occasion he left a lasting impression on me. Despite being an IIT topper, he did not head to some top US university for a master's degree, as many of his batchmates would have. Instead, he set up a startup that leverages technology to address healthcare-related challenges, particularly in our rural areas. He is fiercely committed to this cause and very passionate about it. No wonder his company is such a big success. However, none of these has affected him. He remains extremely humble, with no trace of arrogance or undue pride. I am also told that his company hires a lot of fresh engineers from underprivileged backgrounds as a matter of policy. And there are a whole lot of other social causes that he supports." Virat was effusive about how impressed he was with Rohan.

"Wow!" exclaimed Priya, catching a brief glimpse of Varsha's happy expression, which suggested that she might reconsider her reluctance to meet Rohan.

It was around 6 pm when a hospital staff member walked up to Rajan and said the surgery had been completed successfully, and that Sujata would soon be shifted to her room.

"Can I meet the surgeon, Dr Venkateshwaran?" asked Rajan. "Sorry, sir, but you can meet his assistant, Dr Ashok. Dr Venkateshwaran has left for the Saibaba Hospital, where he consults and treats the poor for free *every evening. A huge crowd normally awaits that keeps him busy until 10 PM," answered the staff member, clearly proud of Dr Venkateshwaran.*

"That is another Karmayogi for you," said Rajan as he set out to meet Dr. Ashok for an update.

Chapter 14

Jnana Yoga - Path of Knowledge and Wisdom

Gaining real knowledge through continuous learning is another route to lasting happiness!

If you are curious and experience a constant quest for knowledge, Jnana Yoga is the path for you. It is the path of knowledge and wisdom which, when internalised and lived, can lead to Ananda through a heightened state of awareness. Jnana Yoga is a path of the intellect. It is a comprehensive practice of self-study to answer such questions as:

- Who am I?

- What is the purpose of my life?

- What is happiness? How can one always be happy?

- Does God exist?

- How can one experience God?

- How does one control one's mind?

- What happens after death?

In Jnana Yoga, the best results are achieved under the guidance of a guru. According to our scriptures, there are certain prerequisites for being a good Jnana yogi (both student and guru). An ideal student should possess the following attributes:

- Concentration, practice, hard work, sincerity, dedication, patience, perseverance and an intense desire for gaining true knowledge.

- A spirit of surrender or complete trust with respect to the guru, attained after a process of **counter-questioning**. [Note how 'questioning the guru' by the student has been made a prerequisite for learning. Such questioning was not merely accepted, but insisted upon as an essential quality in a good student.]

An ideal guru is one who possesses **all the above qualities of a good student** and, in addition,

- is well-versed in Shastras

- is a practitioner of what he preaches

- has a passion for learning continuously

- values service and sacrifice

- is realised

- has the capacity to make others realised

A Jnana yogi must be an extremely open-minded and patient person, with an ability to learn from diverse sources. He should be able to hear and process diverse views and opinions and still prevent his mind from getting overly influenced by ideas that make him forget the very purpose of his seeking.

The process of learning in Jnana Yoga has been split into three stages:

- **Shravanam** or hearing, or receiving the initial inputs. In today's context, reading a book or watching a video could also be classified as Shravanam. This stage results in **Information**.

- **Mananam** or comprehending, or logically understanding what one has read, heard or watched, to either accept or reject the same. This might involve recapitulating the information in one's mind, questioning it to the maximum, and discussing it with the guru and other knowledgeable people until one gets fully convinced in terms of logic. This stage results in **Knowledge**.

- **Nidhidhyasanam** or meditating upon or dwelling upon what one has understood and accepted, and practising it intensely until the knowledge gets internalised and stabilised. This stage results in **Wisdom**.

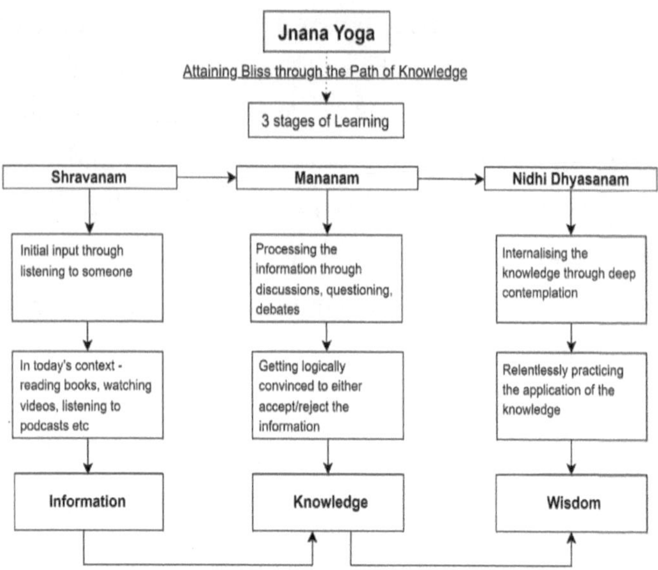

As we go deeper and deeper into meditation with ever-increasing knowledge and wisdom, we start unravelling higher and higher dimensions of existence, until we get convinced that 'I am one with this universe', which is true Jnana or Ananda.

It was a Friday evening, and the TV was abuzz with the news of the arrest of a popular religious figure. This 'self-proclaimed' guru, who had lakhs of followers, had been

found guilty of abusing a girl in his ashram. The disturbing news had got the Rajan family angry.

"If questioning the guru was a key part of the learning process, how come so many Hindus seem to blindly follow fake gurus these days? Weren't several more of these so-called spiritual gurus found guilty of serious crimes by our courts over the last decade?" *asked Virat.*

"You are right," said Rajan, and added, "The Hindu society seems to have forgotten the fact that the followers of Sanatana Dharma are supposed to be seekers, not just blind believers. People accept the authority of gurus so easily these days. This is completely against the spirit of learning described in the Upanishads, which emphasise questioning and personal experience.

"Even Adi Shankara had to establish his ideas through intense debates. His famous debate with another Vedic scholar of his times, Mandana Mishra, which is said to have lasted several days and was presided over by the latter's wife, Ubhaya Bharati, is a great testament to the intellectual rigour that was inherent in the Sanatana Dharma philosophical traditions. In this famous debate, Adi Shankara argued the case of Advaita Vedanta as opposed to the ritualistic school that Mandana Mishra represented. The debate, which had a far-reaching impact on Sanatana Dharma thought, highlights the

importance of Samvada (dialogue) and Vivada (debate) in the quest for knowledge and truth within Sanatana Dharma. Furthermore, the eventual conversion of Mandana Mishra to Advaita Vedanta following the debate shows the openness to new ideas and perspectives within Sanatana Dharma."

The classic debate between Adi Shankara and Mandana Mishra, with the latter's wife playing judge

"A progressive decay over successive generations, actively promoted by vested interests, has led to this state. The fears and anxieties of the common man have been exploited to establish a culture of blind faith in rituals and superstitions over several centuries. Families with a hierarchical approach, where parents

rebuke their children for questioning their ways, have also contributed to this culture of blind following.

"If one were to go by the spirit of 'learning through questioning' described in our scriptures, one should not accept any view from any authority blindly, no matter how high or revered that authority might be. One can receive these inputs, process them in one's own mind without any bias or prejudice, put them to scrutiny through personal experiments, and only if validated, accept them as one's own truth. Spiritual evolution and progress can happen only through such personal effort and experience. In reality though, people do not want to undertake this rigour. They want instant solutions from popular gurus, whose views they accept as absolute truth without any scrutiny whatsoever. Therefore, often the outcomes fall terribly short," asserted Rajan.

"Are you then saying that it is perfectly fine if I do not chant shlokas or visit temples, but pursue life's purpose of ultimate happiness through the process of self-study and personal experiments within myself?" *asked Virat, genuinely curious.*

"That is perfectly fine, provided you follow some core values to lead a good and honourable life. Once we are through with the discussions on all of my notes, you will get a broad idea of the Sanatana Dharma

way of life. I would recommend you consider the same seriously, particularly the recommendations of Karma Yoga, Jnana Yoga, Bhakti Yoga, and Raja Yoga, before embarking on your personal quest for happiness. Else, you may end up spending your whole life reinventing the wheel," said Rajan.

"Let's cross the bridge when we come to it, Appa," *responded Virat, conveying his unwillingness to disclose his views until the discussions were completed on all of Rajan's notes.*

"Reading books and consuming content created by experts in Sanatana Dharma can help one to get started on one's spiritual journey. It could also help to enhance one's knowledge of the subject, but only up to a point. The same applies to following the discourses and recommendations of gurus, however popular they might be. In my view, real knowledge and advancement in spirituality can happen only through personal practice, experiments and experiences. All other sources like books, internet content and self-appointed gurus can only provide inputs for your scrutiny, contemplation and careful consideration, to be eventually either incorporated into your life or to be discarded." Rajan's views sounded very liberating and empowering to both Virat and Varsha.

*"**I shall surely consider the recommendations of the Sanatana way of life, but purely on merit,**" asserted Varsha.*

"A word of caution though. The pursuit of spiritual evolution itself could get addictive. While embarking on this journey, one should be aware of the risk that one might unconsciously end up spending all of one's time in this pursuit and neglecting even one's duties. It is important to guard against this, as the performance of one's duties is supreme and should never be compromised." Priya's remarks betrayed her concern that her young children, driven by the desire of an intense spiritual pursuit, should not end up losing all interest in a normal worldly life.

*"**Appa, learning seems to have been so much more fun during the Vedic era. Today, most of our learning in school and college involves mugging up lots and lots of information. There is not much scope for contemplation and questioning, let alone application and experience.**" Varsha's views were likely to be echoed by most students in India today.*

*"**I simply love the three-step process of learning described in your notes, consisting of Shravanam for information intake, Mananam for understanding the information before accepting it as knowledge, and Nidhidhyasanam for finally internalising the knowledge to make it one's wisdom. I wish we**

followed these steps in all our learning today," said Priya, having clearly read the notes more than once.

"I couldn't agree more. Colonial rule not only impoverished us, but also forced upon us an education system designed to churn out clerks rather than leaders. That did not help matters. It always stopped us at the stage of information gathering, never encouraging us to gain real knowledge or wisdom," said Rajan.

"Can anyone name a great Jnana yogi?" asked Varsha.

"Adi Shankaracharya without any doubt. How he mastered all our scriptures at such a young age, and added so much to our overall body of knowledge through his magnificent commentaries on the scriptures, is quite incredible. He also repeatedly asserted that Maya can be overcome only by knowledge. It is clear, he chose the path of knowledge.' Priya's emphatic and correct assertion left little room for debate.

The TV news was now showing the fake guru being taken to the prison. The Rajan family felt happy seeing the criminal being served his due.

Chapter 15

Bhakti Yoga - Path of Selfless and Pure Love

Developing and remaining in pure love is a sure way to Ananda!

Bhakti Yoga is a path of pure and selfless love.

We are in an era where we have developed our intellect greatly but have not worked on our emotions. The left brain (which is related to logic) is very developed, but the right brain (which is related to emotions) is hardly trained. Selfishness has increased, with little concern or love for others. We want everything for ourselves, even if it means depriving others of what is rightfully theirs. That is why we are stuck with a lot of negative emotions like insecurity, fear, hatred, jealousy, ego, anger and greed.

Culturing of our emotions is the bedrock of Bhakti Yoga. What is an emotion? When a thought is repeated over and over again, it becomes an emotion. This happens when, instead of letting a thought pass us like a cloud, we hold onto it. And when we hold onto a potent thought, it becomes intense and powerful. It then does not remain just at the brain level but goes deep down and becomes an emotion. Speed of thought is the defining feature of intense emotion. Bhakti Yoga helps in channelising one's emotions in the right direction. It helps one to cultivate and develop the emotion of love in oneself, to eventually make it one's default emotion.

Bhakti is deep love for God driven by an intense desire to merge with God. It is nothing but love in its purest form. Through Bhakti, one can transform negative emotions into positive emotions. More specifically, one can convert

- Desire (Kama) to a desire for service
- Greed (Lobha) to a burning ambition to impact the world positively
- Attachment (Moha) to selfless love
- Fear (Bhaya) to the fear of adharma or immoral actions
- Arrogance (Mada) to self-confidence
- Jealousy (Matsarya) to a passion to be the best
- Grief (Shoka) to Empathy

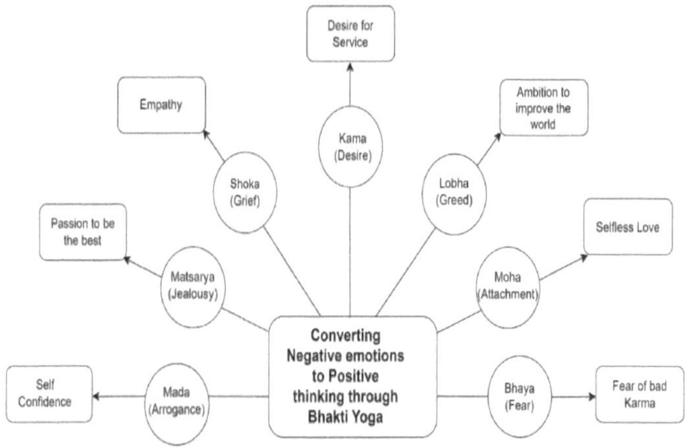

The unique Sanatana Dharma concept of a Personal God is a great vehicle for progress in Bhakti Yoga. Here, the seeker chooses a Personal God (like Shiva, Krishna, Ganesha, Durga) whose form and stories he finds most appealing. The seeker then makes that Personal God the object of his love, respect and admiration, gradually growing and evolving it to the level of Bhakti.

Stages of love leading to Bhakti

* **Kama** ('give and take' or transactional). When two people become friends because of some common desires, interests, likes or dislikes, their relationship is likely to be based on 'give and take'. Example: Two men, both of whom loved playing tennis with each other, became good friends. After a year, one of them got injured and gave up tennis for good. Their

friendship started eroding gradually. There was no real love or friendship here. It was Kama.

- **Prema** (Kama plus sacrifice). This involves giving without the expectation of getting anything in return. The lover gives all material possessions to the beloved. There is no logic to such giving. It is spontaneous. Prema brings great satisfaction and fulfilment, and the mind experiences great calm. Example: A rich man gets friendly with a poor man whose family is in deep financial distress. Over time, their friendship grows so much that the rich man decides to take charge and rid his friend of all his woes. He dedicates his full time and almost his entire wealth to get the friend and his family out of their deep distress. He goes on giving all that he possesses. There is no logic to such giving other than pure friendship and love. This is Prema.

- **Bhakti** (Prema without the feeling of 'I am giving'). In this stage, the bhakta sacrifices not just material or bodily possessions, but also his ego. In this state, all strong likes and dislikes, hatred and obsessions, fears and moodiness of the bhakta vanish. Here the bhakta gets expanded to an all-pervasive eternal divinity, losing individuality and reaching a state of complete merger with his personal God. As the bhakta surrenders totally to God, he finds God everywhere and in everything. God blesses the bhakta with all that he might want. However, all that the bhakta wants at this stage is God. When all desires are gone, all desires are 'fulfilled'!! Example: Meerabai (for Lord Krishna), Ramakrishna Paramahamsa (for Goddess Kali).

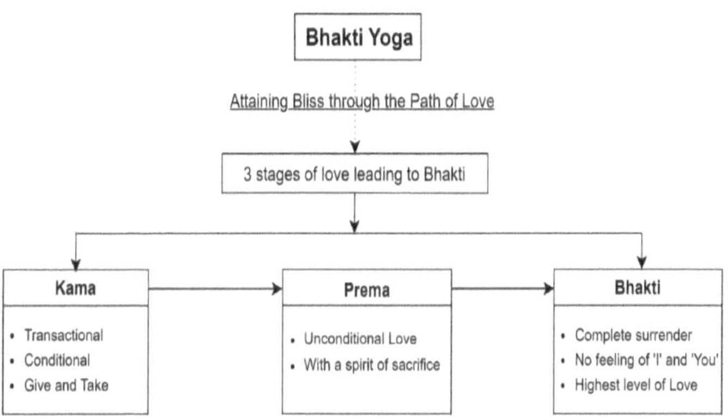

Bhakti Yoga recognises five types of emotions that a Bhakta can have towards God.

- Dasya Bhava (servant-master like Hanuman-Rama or student-teacher like Arjuna-Krishna)

- Madhurya Bhava (lovers like Radha-Krishna)

- Vatsalya Bhava (parent-child like Yashoda-Krishna)

- Sakhya Bhava (friends like Sudama-Krishna)

- Shanta Bhava (steady, serene, peaceful feeling of love and contentment without any disturbance or distraction, like Bhishma-Krishna. Though circumstances placed Bhishma in Krishna's enemy camp during the Mahabharata war, Bhishma was deeply aware of Krishna's divinity and maintained an unwavering devotion to Krishna till his last breath)

This freedom to imagine one's relationship with God in various ways is unique to Sanatana Dharma. Chapter XI, verse 44 of the Bhagavad Gita says:

तस्मात्प्रणम्य प्रणिधाय कायं

प्रसादये त्वामहमीशमीड्यम्।

पितेव पुत्रस्य सखेव सख्यु: प्रिय: प्रियायार्हसि देव सोढुम्॥

tasmāt praṇamya praṇidhāya kāyaṁ

prasādaye tvām aham īśham īḍyam

piteva putrasya sakheva sakhyuḥ

priyaḥ priyaayārhasi deva soḍhum

Translation

"Therefore, bowing down, prostrating my body, I crave your forgiveness, adorable Lord. As a father forgiveth his son, a friend his friend, a lover his beloved, even so should you forgive me, O DEVA." [The Holy Geeta, Commentary by Swami Chinmayananda][9]

Here, Arjuna, after realising that the person he was interacting with so far as a close friend was, in fact, God himself, seeks pardon from Krishna for any transgressions that might have occurred from his side owing to his lack of knowledge about Krishna's real identity. And then he goes on to say that

---

9 From Swami Chinmayananda's commentary on the Bhagavad Gita, in a book titled "The Holy Geeta"

Krishna should forgive him just as a parent would forgive his child, a friend his friend, and a lover his beloved. This verse again brings out the freedom that Sanatana Dharma provides to its followers to imagine their relationship with God in the manner that they find maximum happiness and peace in.

Bhakti Yoga speaks of nine techniques to create, nurture, and grow Bhakti in oneself. These are

- Shravanam: Hearing about God

- Kirtanam: Singing the praise of God

- Smaranam: Remembering God

- Paada Sevanam: Worshipping the feet of God

- Archana: Worshipping the various images of God

- Vandanam: Salutations to God

- Dasyam: Service of God

- Sakhyam: Friendship with God

- Atma Nivedanam: Complete Surrender to God

Priya's 78-year-old mother, fondly referred to as Ammamma by the Rajan family, had come on a visit. Ammamma was remarkably fit and agile for her age. She had two passions which were the real anchors in her life. One was her daily

puja to a small Krishna idol that she carried with her even when she travelled. She spent hours in her puja for the idol that she did twice a day. She had never missed this routine even once for over a decade now. And the other passion was cooking and feeding her children and grandchildren.

There was a remarkable selflessness in Ammamma's second passion. While she cooked exquisitely, she seldom ate her exotic preparations. She had restricted her own diet to just fruits and two cups of porridge every day. Exceptions were few and far between.

Ammamma was popular among all her three children and their families, and this was in no small measure attributable to her second passion, besides, of course, her extremely amiable and loving nature.

It was lunchtime on a Saturday, and the Rajan family was waiting impatiently at the dining table to gorge on an elaborate meal that Ammamma had cooked for the family. She was in the puja room, offering the dessert that she had prepared as prasad to her Krishna idol. The family was waiting for the puja to be over before starting to eat.

"Lata had called me yesterday. She was suggesting we have the wedding in early February. Her family priest has suggested 2nd February. It is supposedly an auspicious date. What do you all say?" *asked Priya. Lata was Virat's girlfriend Neha's mother.*

"Hold on. I am fine with getting married on any date, but I do not want a traditional wedding with all the rituals. I would prefer just a court wedding, followed by a reception for close friends and relatives," Virat's reaction was swift and clear.

"Oh, come on, Virat. I agree that it is your wedding and you should have the primary say. That said, the two immediate families too have a right to celebrate this once-in-a-lifetime event. I know that both parents of Neha would feel more comfortable with a traditional wedding ceremony. I too cannot wait to see the two of you in the splendour of our traditional wedding attires," said Priya, putting forth a strong reason why Virat should change his position.

"After all, the rituals last just half a day and are a lot of fun for the family. They leave us with memories for a lifetime," said Rajan in support of his wife.

"No, Appa. The families can have all their fun during the evening reception. I really wish to avoid the traditional rituals. I see it as a waste of time and money," said Virat, expressing his considered view.

"What about Neha? What does she want?" Varsha was clearly unhappy that Virat was deciding on the matter unilaterally. **"She disagreed to begin with, but is now reasonably aligned with me on this matter,"** said Virat.

"*Ammamma will be heartbroken with this decision of yours. Ever since she came to know about the wedding, she has been very excited. She has been speaking about all the traditional events, the role each relative plays, and the gifts we need to give them for the same,*" *said Priya in a tone filled with regret. This was followed by a few minutes of silence, with Virat pretending to check some messages on his phone, and Priya deciding to discuss this in private with Virat later.*

A few minutes later, the family was feasting. Ammamma was fasting that day and had retired to her room after her puja. Everyone was enchanted by the food. Each dish was better than the other.

"How does she do it at this age?" *asked a wonderstruck Varsha.*

"If you ask her, she will say it is all her Krishna's blessing," *answered Priya.*

The banter that followed almost seamlessly moved into a discussion on Bhakti Yoga.

"Bhakti Yoga appeals to me. Just going into our puja room brings about a feeling of peace in me. I find peace in the act of lighting the lamp, chanting my shlokas, and offering flowers and prasad to the pictures of our different Gods.

"What I derive is strength. A sense of security that we are cared for and will be taken care of. And anytime I am anxious or worried about something, I can just pour my heart out without being worried about how I am saying it. I always come out of our puja room with my confidence enhanced," said Priya.

"I am not surprised. Women who have experienced motherhood have a fairly evolved love emotion. They are already conditioned by their motherhood experience to be capable of selfless love. These are my personal views though." Rajan's observation appeared to be based on sound logic.

"I simply loved to read about the five types of emotions which a Bhakta can have towards his Personal God. More than anything else, this brings out the clear intent behind the concept of Personal God, and the various forms that we worship. It is so easy to see a good friend in the personalities of Ganesha and Hanuman, as described in our mythology. Imagine having a friend with a sense of commitment like Hanuman!" Varsha seemed to be reimagining her relationship with her Gods.

"Once you understand the spirit behind the concept of a Personal God, you would also understand the rationale behind the fantastic forms and stories that our mythology provides us with. It makes it so easy to *cultivate and develop the emotions of trust and love for one or more of those forms that resonate the most with your own personality and station in life."*

"The stories make it easy to develop love for God. Depending on your own likes and dislikes, you are very likely to take a liking to one or more of those forms," explained Rajan.

"Would Bhakti Yoga rank lower than other Yogas because of its reliance on so many forms and rituals?" *queried Virat.*

"On the contrary, I would rank Bhakti Yoga very highly. It is Bhakti Yoga that has made Sanatana Dharma so accessible to the common man."

"The concept of Bhakti or intense devotion, and the way it is nurtured and grown, is quite unique to Sanatana Dharma. Almost every Hindu household has a separate space reserved for the Gods, where each member of the family engages every day with their Personal God with deep emotion by lighting lamps and incense sticks, offering flowers and sweets, and so on. This deep personal bond gets strengthened more and more every day, irrespective of the existence or otherwise of public places of worship like temples. In my view, this is the biggest reason why Sanatana Dharma has survived for thousands of years, despite so many challenges."

"Can you name someone whom you regard as a great exponent of Bhakti Yoga?" asked Virat, ever so keen to associate these concepts with a known face.

"To my mind, Ramakrishna Paramahamsa, the guru of Swami Vivekananda, was a Bhakti yogi. If you go back further, you have Meerabai whose total love for Krishna can only be described as Bhakti Yoga," said Rajan, adding further in a somewhat contemplative tone, "I suspect there would be many more Bhakti yogis, whom we may have never heard of. And for all you know, our own Ammamma too might have covered a considerable distance in her Bhakti Yoga journey." Rajan's last sentence brought a smile of approval to the other three faces.

Meera Bai   Ramakrishna Paramahamsa

Chapter 16

Raja Yoga - Path of Willpower and Mind Control

Gaining mastery over the mind through determined and relentless work on oneself is a proven method to attain Ananda.

Raja Yoga is the path of willpower, most suited for the strong-willed person. It is literally like a process manual to tame the mind and attain Ananda! Raja Yoga encompasses both body and mind, but the emphasis is more on mental development. It aims at gaining mastery over the mind.

Raja Yoga is based on Patanjali's Ashtanga Yoga (the eight-limbed Yoga), which proposes two broad tracks - *Bahiranga* Yoga and *Antaranga* Yoga.

Bahiranga* Yoga** is an indirect method to gain mastery over the mind. It consists of five action areas, namely ***Yama, Niyama, Asana, Pranayama and Pratyahara.

Yamas (Don'ts)

* *Ahimsa* (non-violence) in thoughts, words, and actions;

* *Satya* (honesty or integrity) - avoiding falsehood and shunning dishonesty, to align one's thoughts, words and actions with truth;

* *Asteya* (non-stealing) - not seeking what is not yours. Not being covetous or envious;

* Brahmacharya: not being a slave to your senses;

* *Aparigraha* - non-hoarding, or avoiding the excessive accumulation of material objects;

Niyama (Do's)

* *Shaucha* (cleanliness) - both external and internal purity. According to our Shastras, just as water can purify the body, truthfulness can purify the mind, while true knowledge can purify the intellect.

* *Santosha* (contentment) - to be content with what one has earned the rightful way and through honest means. This involves the practice of gratitude and maintaining equanimity through all that life offers.

- *Tapas* (austerity) - developing the power to withstand hardships like thirst, hunger, cold and heat;

- *Swadhyaya* (introspection) - to do self-study, reflect, introspect and constantly improve;

- *Ishvara Pranidhana* or surrender to the divine, which will neutralise the ego;

Asana

- Physical exercises like Yoga Asanas to strengthen the body and keep it healthy;

Pranayama

- Exercises to regulate the breath and calm the mind using the breath.

Pratyahara

- Developing a degree of detachment to overcome negative attributes like insecurity, fear, hatred, jealousy, ego, anger and greed. Such detachment can help one to maintain moderation in the pursuit of sensory pleasures, so as not to become enslaved by them.

Antaranga Yoga or the direct method to gain mastery over the mind through intense meditation. This involves three steps or stages of mind control, namely Dharana,

Dhyana and Samadhi. Here we use our intellect to directly control and tame the mind.

Dharana

- This is the first stage of direct control over the mind. Generally there are umpteen thoughts floating in the mind. With concentration, it can be brought down to a single thought. This is the stage of Dharana, which essentially involves concentration or intense focus on any one object or thought.

Dhyana

- This is the second stage of direct control over the mind. It is a stage when one becomes comfortable in Dharana. Dhyana is effortless Dharana. If Dharana is intense and unwavering focus, then Dhyana is some sort of de-focusing that removes the effort from Dharana. It is the stage when focus becomes effortless and pleasurable. You feel like staying in this state. It is a state of deep concentration and effortless detachment at the same time.

  At this stage, though, the three entities, namely the seer (the person meditating), the seen (the object of meditation), and the seeing (the process of meditation), still retain their independence and separateness.

Samadhi

- This is the third stage of direct control over the mind. Here all the three entities, namely, the seer (the person meditating), the seen (the object of meditation), and the seeing (the process of meditation), merge into one. Only the experience prevails at this stage. It is a jump into inner consciousness, a whole new world, a state of Ananda.

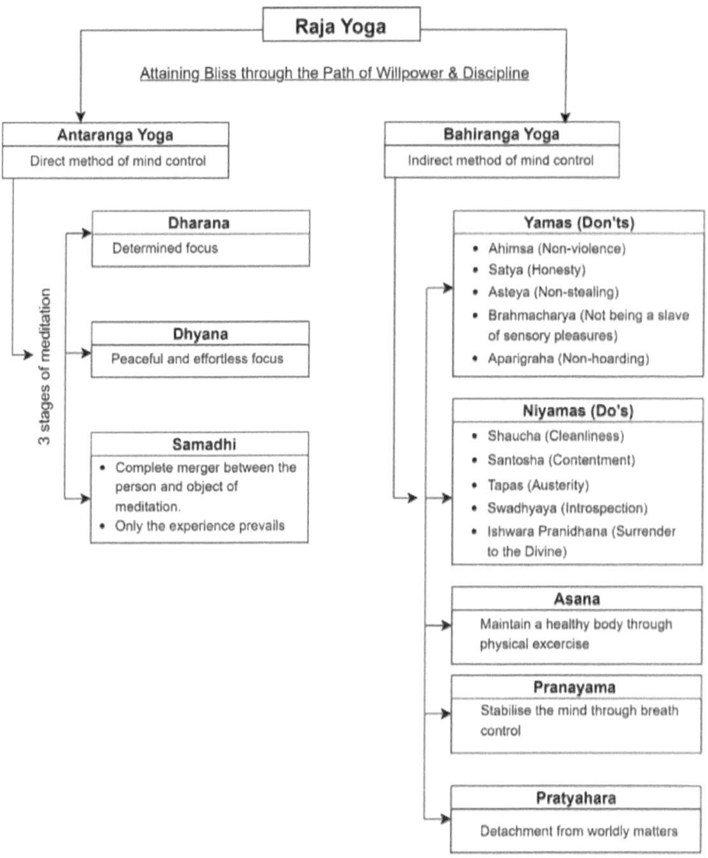

It was the death anniversary of Rajan's father as per the Hindu calendar and, as was customary in the Rajan household, three priests had arrived in the morning to conduct the annual Shradh ceremony and related rituals. While Rajan did go to work that day, thoughts pertaining to his late father cropped up quite a few times in his mind.

Rajan's father, an engineer by qualification, did quite well in his career as a Sales Manager in a private firm. However, most of what he earned went towards meeting the wedding expenses of his daughters. His life had been full of challenges, both on the personal and professional fronts. Despite this, he maintained his equanimity. He was a man of few words and was deeply spiritual. He would spend hours every day in his puja and meditation.

Rajan was the last but one among eight siblings, and the only son. There was a big age gap between him and his father. There was hardly any communication between them during Rajan's school and college days. It was only when Rajan was past twenty-five that meaningful interactions started taking place between them. Unfortunately, by the time Rajan turned 31, his father was no more. Not having communicated adequately with his father was a major regret in Rajan's life. How he wished he had had the good sense to spend more time with his father in his late teens and early twenties. He could have learnt so much more.

It was while Rajan was in the middle of such sombre thoughts that the discussion on Rajan's note on Raja Yoga started between Priya, Virat, and Varsha. It took a few minutes for Rajan to tune in mentally.

"Raja Yoga sounds a little highbrow to me. I find the concept of Dhyana, or effortless and pleasurable focus on the object of meditation, difficult to imagine. I find it so hard to focus without interruption, even for a minute," *observed Virat.*

"I think my father reached the Dhyana stage. I have seen him sit still in meditation, in peace, for over an hour every day. And he seemed to enjoy it, for that was the first thing he would do on return from a day's hard work." Rajan's admiration for his father was evident.

"Perhaps that was the reason why he could always maintain such calm, despite the tough challenges that life threw at him. In my childhood, I have also seen him bear unreal levels of physical pain. Once my parents and I went to an evening puja in our neighbourhood in Kolkata. It must have been the early 1970s. By the time the puja drew towards an end, it was past ten. As a part of the closing rituals, a plate full of burning camphor, used for the aarti, was being taken around the room to each devotee, all of whom were sitting on the floor. Suddenly the plate slipped from the hands of the person and fell on my father's back, which was bare and sweating profusely because of the heat. The plate fell off, but the entire lot of burning camphor stuck to my father's wet back. It was a gory sight, and my mother almost fainted. Shortly thereafter the three of us had to

walk back to our home because we just could not find any other mode of transport at that hour. Not an 'ouch' from my father, as he led the walk briskly, with the two of us following him back home. The extensive burns on his back took several months to heal thereafter."

"Do you think he was pursuing Raja Yoga?" *asked Virat, curious to know more about his grandfather.*

"I think he was following multiple paths. I have seen him not only in states of deep meditation, but also in states of deep Bhakti, overwhelmed completely with love for his Personal Gods. After his demise, I chanced upon what he had written in his personal diary about his pilgrimage to the Amarnath cave in the Himalayas. He had written quite eloquently about how he went into a trance-like state when he set his eyes on the Ice Shivling in the cave and could perceive nothing other than his God. It read as though he experienced a state of complete merger or Ananda in those moments."

"Whatever he was doing to manage his mind clearly worked for him. He was always calm and unruffled. Today, whenever I think of him, I feel so proud, yet also regretful that I could not spend more time with him." Rajan's emotions drew instant empathy from the other three.

"*As far as you and Varsha are concerned, if you try meditating for at least 15 minutes every day for a year, I think you will start enjoying it and transition successfully from Dharana to Dhyana. You will also experience the benefits of a much better state of mind in all aspects of your life.*" Rajan was keen to see his children practise some form of meditation regularly for their overall well-being and success.

"And the concept of Samadhi, which speaks of the meditator, the object of meditation, and the act of meditating all merging into one unified experience, is beyond my imagination. I am unable to imagine what such a state would be, and whether it is even possible to attain such a state!" exclaimed Virat.

"*Samadhi is a different level of meditation altogether. Many of our great sages and saints like Swami Vivekananda have reached that stage.*"

"What are the types of people most suited to pursue Raja Yoga?" *asked Varsha.*

"*People with strong willpower would be most suited for Raja Yoga. This is a path wherein one is continuously working on oneself, through Yoga Asanas for the body, Pranayama for the breath and life energies, and intense meditation for the mind and intellect. It calls for great discipline and determined effort.*"

Paramahansa Yogananda, the author of the bestseller 'An Autobiography of a Yogi', the book that inspired Steve Jobs, was a famous Raja Yogi."

Swami Vivekananda   Paramahansa Yogananda

Chapter 17

Inaction Is Not an Option

*Staying away from action, in a bid to escape
from the reaction to Karma, is not an option.*

Discussions on Raja Yoga, the method of intense meditation, often give rise to the question, "Should I just walk away from my familiar world, retire to a lonely place and isolate myself, so that I can work on my mind and meditate without any distraction?" The Bhagavad Gita answers that question with a categorical 'No'. Since the performance of one's duties is of paramount importance, there is no question of walking away from one's duties towards one's family and society.

In fact, our day-to-day life, with all its distractions, presents the best setting for us to work on our mind and build our mental strength. The challenges of a worldly life provide us with the best opportunity to practise mental drills like Sakshi Bhava or 'witnessing the mind' and evaluate their effectiveness in coping with those challenges. Therefore, inaction is not an option.

Chapter III, verse 8 of the Bhagavad Gita says

नियतं कुरु कर्म त्वं कर्म ज्यायो ह्यकर्मण:।
शरीरयात्रापि च ते न प्रसिद्ध्येदकर्मण:॥

niyataṁ kuru karma tvaṁ karma jyāyo hyakarmaṇaḥ
śharīra-yātrāpi cha te na prasiddhyed akarmaṇaḥ

Translation

"You perform your bounden duty; for action is superior to inaction. Even the maintenance of the body would not be possible for you by inaction." [The Holy Geeta, Commentary by Swami Chinmayananda][10]

Life is not for mere existence. The gift of life should be used to accomplish and to make a positive impact around us. Chasing accomplishments, though, would result in more Karma, some right and some wrong. This means that the reactions to these Karma too would need to be exhausted before one attains Ananda and gets liberated from the cycle of births and deaths. Therefore, some persons seeking

---

10 From Swami Chinmayananda's commentary on the Bhagavad Gita, in a book titled "The Holy Geeta"

Ananda may desist from action itself for the fear of adding more Karma, which would then have to be exhausted through further experiences. According to the Bhagavad Gita, such an approach would be a misguided one and would yield no results. The right approach would be to do one's Karma with the attitude of a Karmayogi and evolve oneself.

Chapter XVIII, verse 8 of the Bhagavad Gita says

दु:खमित्येव यत्कर्म कायक्लेशभयात्यजेत्।
स कृत्वा राजसं त्यागं नैव त्यागफलं लभेत्॥

duḥkham ity eva yat karma kāya-kleśa-bhayāt tyajet
sa kṛitvā rājasaṁ tyāgaṁ naiva tyāga-phalaṁ labhet

Translation

"Abandoning prescribed duties due to physical discomfort or because they are troublesome is renunciation driven by passion. Such renunciation can never be beneficial or uplifting."

Some people use the excuse of spiritual pursuit and renunciation to escape from their duties that might be difficult and uncomfortable to perform. Such renunciation or spiritual pursuit is nothing more than escaping from the challenges of life and is hence wrong. It will yield no benefit.

Arjuna knew he could survive even without his kingdom and all the material pleasures that accompanied it. Engaging in war would entail emotional and physical hardship. So, his question as to why he should go to war was, in some sense, legitimate. The Lord's response was that notwithstanding the fact that there might be an easier way out of a problem, if it doesn't do justice to all concerned, one can't opt for it. We owe a debt of duty by virtue of our station in life, and that has to be repaid by the right action.

"Your note on inaction is confusing. If Raja Yoga, the path of intense meditation through Dhyana, Dharana and Samadhi, can lead us to Ananda, what is wrong if a man retires from engaging with the world and goes into solitude to pursue the Raja Yoga prescriptions?" asked Virat.

"If you need to develop the mental strength to make your mind distraction-proof, running away from distractions is not the answer. Even if you spend years working on your mind in solitude, how would you know whether your efforts have actually strengthened your mind? The only way to test that would be to return to the material world and check whether you can now maintain equanimity in the midst of the very challenges that distracted and disturbed you earlier," countered Rajan.

"How then can one pursue Ananda efficiently and speedily in the middle of this chaotic world?" asked Varsha.

"By using the day-to-day chaos itself as a drill. Like I have said before, the four paths (Karma Yoga, Jnana Yoga, Bhakti Yoga, and Raja Yoga) are not mutually exclusive. No matter which of these four paths you choose as your predominant driver of growth, you would still have elements of the other three in your life. Accordingly, even if you have chosen Raja Yoga as your primary path, you should still approach your worldly actions in the spirit of Karma Yoga."

"This would involve learning to enjoy giving your best for honourable goals, without worrying about outcomes. You should learn to enjoy your work through the use of stimulating goals, creative plans, intense efforts, smart execution, etc., without getting obsessive about results."

"And you should train yourself to maintain your equanimity through both success and failures. And for this, you would need to use all the techniques prescribed in our scriptures for mind management, like witnessing the mind and meditation. These techniques have been discussed in greater detail in a subsequent set of notes."

"And when you succeed in managing your mind flawlessly even in the face of all the trials and tribulations of worldly life, there can be no doubt about your progress and evolution," said an eloquent Rajan.

"Rajan, you have made the common man's day-to-day life itself sound like the most fun-filled and exciting challenge one can possibly take up," said a smiling Priya, clearly in admiration of her husband's articulation skills.

"Talking about inaction, Amma and Appa, can the two of you also shake this sister of mine out of her inaction with respect to finding a good husband for herself," said Virat with a smile.

"I agree, Varsha. I repeat you should seriously consider connecting with Rohan. I see no logic in your refusing to do so unless you are already seeing someone. I know you desire a happy married and family life. Why then are you refusing to meet someone I feel would be great for you? I don't understand the reason for this inaction. Is it a fear of possible rejection?" Priya asked Varsha, who responded merely with a smile and a shrug of her shoulders.

"I know she met a person whom her colleague had recommended. It did not progress because she did not like that interaction," Virat's comments were met with an angry stare from Varsha. "That is why I am unable to understand why not Rohan? I know him and find him very impressive," continued Virat. The protective elder brother was keen to see Varsha in a stable relationship, preferably leading to marriage, before flying off to the

US. So was Priya. Rajan, on the other hand, wanted no pressure to be exerted on Varsha on this matter.

"Really? So you are open to meeting someone suggested by a person whom you have known for barely a couple of years, but not someone suggested by your near and dear ones who have known you and cared for you your whole life! Strange, to say the least," said a clearly frustrated Priya.

"Amma, the person Virat is referring to is not a stranger. He is my colleague Reema's cousin. We met once at a coffee shop, but neither of us felt like progressing that any further."

"I know you care for me more than anyone else, but that does not mean you would know the sort of person I want as my life partner. The world has changed completely since you got married. What makes a relationship work today is very different from what it used to be 30 years back," said Varsha.

"But I have spent more time with you than anyone has till now, and that makes me reasonably qualified to figure out what might work for you, and what might not. No matter where a prospect comes from, the final decision regarding how you wish to proceed is always going to be yours. Given this, I am unable to understand what prevents you from applying your evaluation process on Rohan, just as you would with any other prospect you may meet?" countered Priya, adding, "you are just limiting your options with your stupid self-imposed restrictions."

"I think she does not want to be seen in her social circle as one who chose the route of arranged marriage for securing a life partner. It just does not sound cool enough," said Virat, trying to provoke Varsha into a response.

"Why are we constantly seeking validation from others for all our decisions? We should trust our own intellect and judgement. Your friends are fine with exploring relationships with strangers suggested by dating apps, but averse to meeting someone suggested by parents. I find this approach totally bereft of logic," said Priya, continuing to argue her point.

"We can pause this topic for now," said Rajan, while adding, "That said, I do believe that trying to find a good life partner for oneself is an extremely important and honourable goal. It is arguably the most important decision one takes in one's life. If you get it right, it can empower you greatly, contribute immensely to your success, and fill your life with happiness. While it is generally the heart that feels the initial attraction towards any person, the process of figuring out whether the person is right for you needs to be driven a lot using the head. So Varsha, if you are not meeting promising prospects merely because of the discomfort involved in *the process, or how some of your friends may view your approach, I suggest you reconsider your position. As my notes on 'Inaction' say, avoiding a necessary action because of the discomfort or difficulty involved amounts to escapism that can only cause harm in the long run."*

Mind Management - the Defining Essence of Hindu Philosophy

Working on your own mind is the smartest thing you can possibly do!

One of the greatest contributions of Sanatana Dharma to mankind is its deep study of the human mind and its different states of consciousness, resulting in its clear and unambiguous message that our success, health and happiness depend almost entirely on how we manage our mind. The world is increasingly accepting this now. Today, several experts in medical science seem to be of the view that a majority of our diseases are psychosomatic (caused by the mind), and much less are pathogenic (caused by external invasion of bacteria or virus). Stress is seen to be a primary reason for several psychological and physiological problems.[11]

Irrespective of the above, it is our primary duty to maintain a positive and happy state of mind and to spread that positivity all around. All other forms of social service are secondary. If one's own state of mind is miserable, one can only spread sadness and negativity all around. Therefore, our foremost duty is to always stay happy and peaceful. Our scriptures prescribe specific techniques to achieve this.

According to Sanatana Dharma, the key to a happy and successful life lies in the way we think. Efficient and effective thinking is a skill that can be practised and perfected. In this context, it is important to remember that our scriptures see the mind and intellect as distinct from each other. While the mind triggers and harbours the emotions, it is the intellect that discriminates between right and wrong.

---

11 Cause & effect diagram that illustrates how every organ & system in our body is affected by the mind: https://www.pm-powerconsulting.com/blog/dealing-with-fearwork/

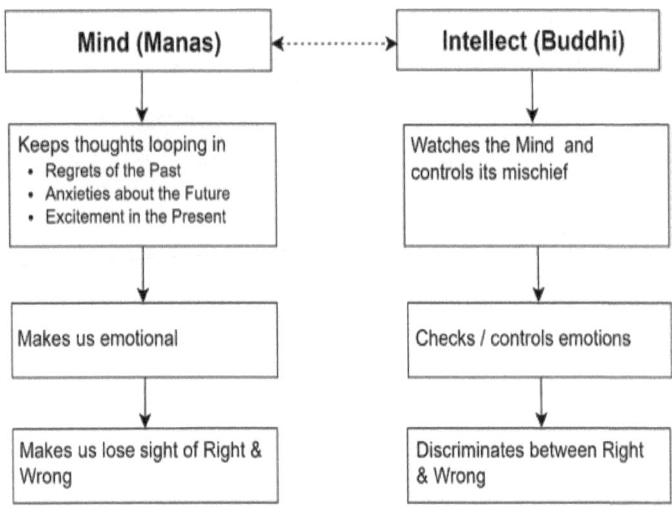

Remember the analogy of a chariot pulled by five horses that we spoke about in a previous chapter titled 'Who Am I'? Each horse represents one of the five senses: sight, hearing, smell, taste and touch. The horses, powerful and restless, constantly pull the reins (our mind) in different directions (towards external objects of temporary pleasures). The charioteer, who controls the reins, symbolises our intellect, while the passenger symbolises our real self or Atman. If the charioteer (intellect) is alert and skilful, he can control the horses (senses) using the reins (mind) and take the passenger (Atman) to the destination (Ananda). This represents a person whose intellect governs the mind, leading to thoughtful decisions and a successful, happy life. However, if the charioteer (intellect) is unwatchful, the horses would run wild pulling the chariot in different directions. This symbolises a person with an uncontrolled mind, which is a sure recipe for stress and frustration.

An uncontrolled mind keeps wallowing in three types of repetitive thoughts: the regrets of the past, the anxieties about the future and excitement in the present. This causes it to experience negative emotions like insecurity, fear, hatred, jealousy, ego, anger and greed, all of which cause stress. Stress leads to haphazard breathing, which in turn affects the metabolic process, resulting in disease. Stress is entirely mind-induced and can be reduced by slowing down one's mind.

A person in rage is the best example of the mind playing havoc. In such an emotion-charged state, perceptions and judgement go completely haywire, making the person say and do things that damage lives and relationships. Therefore, proactive management of the mind is the key to a happy and successful life. Patanjali, the great Indian sage who authored the Yoga Sutras about 2,000 years ago, described Yoga as 'Chitta Vritti Nirodha', which means that Yoga is essentially the calming and stilling of the mind.

Mind management techniques as per Sanatana Dharma

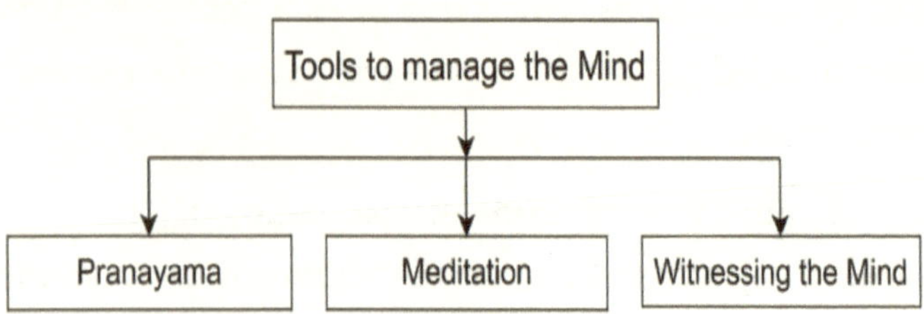

Pranayama

Pranayama or regulated breathing keeps the body and mind in harmony. Our respiratory system is a bridge between the body and the mind, the voluntary and involuntary, the conscious and subconscious. In Pranayama, we voluntarily regulate the breathing rate and balance the breath between the two nostrils. Pranayama involves focus and has a calming effect on the mind. It can work as a good preparatory step before meditation. As an additional benefit, Pranayama also improves the functioning of our respiratory system, enhances lung capacity, and helps in controlling respiratory allergies. Different techniques of Pranayama have been advocated by saints and gurus through the ages. These are easily accessible.

Meditation

Meditation is the most fundamental tool to work on one's mind.

According to our scriptures, meditation is being in the moment, free of thoughts, yet aware. Therefore, both a **thought-free state** and **awareness** are key to meditation. The elimination of thoughts when the mind is still, silent and yet fully alert results in real happiness. Ananda is experienced in this state of thought extinction. It is a state when the mind is totally transcended.

Can our mind be trained in such a way that by default it remains in this state of silence, while being fully conscious and aware (so as to be able to spring into 'thinking' whenever required)? Most certainly, say our scriptures, calling it the highest state of evolution and happiness of a human being.

Meditation is not 'going to sleep'. You need to be alert in meditation. Whenever the mind wanders, you need to 'catch hold of it' and bring it back to whatever you are meditating upon. In the initial stages of practice, the number of times an alert intellect is able to 'catch' the wandering mind and 'bring it back' could itself be viewed as a measure of one's success in meditation.

Meditation can be perfected by relentless practice. The form, activity, or thought that you meditate upon is entirely left to you. With practice, one starts to feel the benefits of meditation. One feels alert and calm at the same time, essentially reflecting the best possible state of one's intellect and mind, respectively.

The most basic technique is to sit in a comfortable position and to focus on one's breath. After the first few minutes of slow and relaxed breathing, one can withdraw all efforts from breathing and just observe and feel the breath go in and out.

Rhythmic sounds, music, and mantras can have a calming effect on the mind. This has been proved beyond doubt by research. These can be very useful tools for effective conditioning of the mind, as preparation for meditation, and even for meditation itself.

Different techniques of meditation have been advocated by saints and gurus through the ages. Almost all of them involve the following stages:

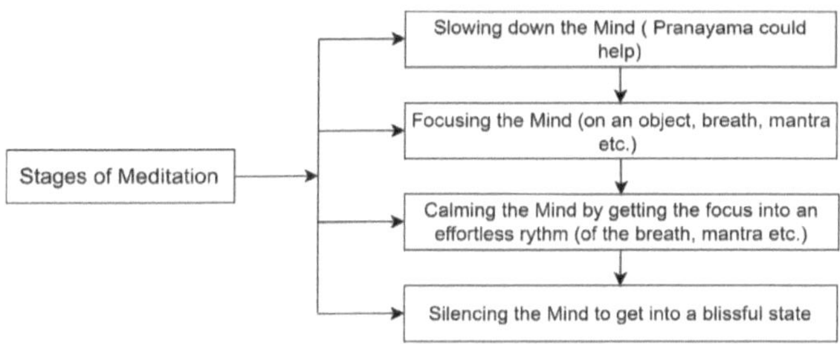

Sakshi Bhava or Witnessing the Mind

How can we ensure that it is our intellect that remains in charge of our thoughts, and not our mind? This requires the development and practice of *'Sakshi Bhava'* or a 'witness mode' of mental state.

Sakshi Bhava is often described as a state of 'being mindful' or 'Mindfulness'. It is an extremely practical approach to deal with the constant mischief played by our mind. Essentially, this is nothing but moderating our thoughts (and thus our words and actions) with a high degree of self-awareness. In this witness mode, we observe our thoughts and emotions, even as they arise and play out in our mind. In other words, we see ourselves as distinct from our mind and do not get identified with it.

Sakshi Bhava helps us remain connected with the here and now and acts as a restraining watchdog over our thoughts whenever they threaten to spiral out of control. It helps us to ensure that our mind does not get swept away by excessively negative emotions like insecurity, fear, hatred, jealousy, ego, anger and greed.

Mindfulness techniques are being increasingly adopted by several leading global companies to enhance employee productivity and to develop leadership skills. Google, for instance, has a programme called 'Search Inside Yourself' (SIY) involving Mindfulness practises based on emotional intelligence and neuroscience evidence. The company has, through a collaboration with Stanford University, established research-based evidence of the positive impact of Mindfulness on human functioning. Several other organisations like SAP, Ford, Apple, LinkedIn, Salesforce, Intel, etc., are adopting Mindfulness practises now.[12]

Swami Chinmayananda in his book *Kindle Life* beautifully describes this process of controlling one's mind using the technique of Sakshi Bhava: "When the mind is uncontrollably agitated and runs about wildly, we can, identifying ourselves with our intellect, watch in perfect detachment the mind in a spirit of sympathetic criticism! The mind may still wander for some time in its own self-appointed fields of activity, but it realises that it is directly under the observation of an uninterested intellect, critically and continuously observing it from the towers of discrimination, and it

---

12 "Search Inside Yourself" by Chade-Meng Tan. eBook Mindfulness@ Work by Vishweshwar Hegde

becomes, as it were, self-conscious and ashamed of itself and retires from its questionable vocations and nestles itself at the feet of the intellect....This technique is called, in our *Śāstras*, the technique of 'Witnessing mind' (*sākṣi-bhāva*)."[13]

It is possible to practise Sakshi Bhava and make it a part of our nature over time. The goal of such practice is to reach a stage wherein this state of witnessing and being aware of one's own mind and its activities comes naturally and eventually becomes one's default state.

Sakshi Bhava creates the right extent of detachment within us, which helps us to experience maximum enjoyment in life. This is akin to a neutral spectator who, free from the pressures of performance, enjoys a good football match much more than the players themselves do.

In Summary

- Working on one's mind is more important than anything else that you can possibly do to achieve sustained happiness.

- The following verses (Chapter VI, verses 5 and 6) from the Bhagavad Gita bring out the importance of working on the mind brilliantly:

---

13 From Swami Chinmayananda's book "Kindle Life"

उद्धरेदात्मनात्मानं नात्मानमवसादयेत्।
आत्मैव ह्यात्मनो बन्धुरात्मैव रिपुरात्मनः॥

बन्धुरात्मात्मनस्तस्य येनात्मैवात्मना जितः।
अनात्मनस्तु शत्रुत्वे वर्ते तात्मैव शत्रुवत्॥

uddhared ātmanātmānaṁ nātmānam avasādayet
ātmaiva hyātmano bandhur ātmaiva ripur ātmanaḥ

bandhur ātmātmanas tasya yenātmaivātmanā jitaḥ
anātmanas tu śhatrutve vartetātmaiva śhatru-vat

Translation

"Use the power of your mind to uplift yourself and not to lower yourself, because the mind can be both your friend and your enemy."

"Those who master their minds find it their friend, while those who fail to do so find it their foe."

Failure to achieve and sustain the highest levels of happiness or Ananda is always on account of a failure to handle one's mind. While we could blame a number of factors for our failures, like our circumstances, lack of resources, or the absence of a good guru, true introspection would always reveal that an uncontrolled mind is our biggest enemy. Therefore, the mind becomes the best friend for those who can tame it and becomes the worst enemy for those who fail to do so.

To bring the mind under the control of the intellect is not easy, but can be achieved by determined efforts, as this verse (Chapter VI, verse 35) from the Bhagavad Gita says:

श्रीभगवानुवाच।
असंशयं महाबाहो मनो दुर्निग्रहं चलम्।
अभ्यासेन तु कौन्तेय वैराग्येण च गृह्यते॥

shrī bhagavān uvācha

asanshayaṁ mahā-bāho mano durnigrahaṁ chalam

abhyāsena tu kaunteya vairāgyeṇa cha gṛihyate

Translation

Lord Krishna said, "O mighty-armed son of Kunti, what you say is indeed true; controlling the mind is very difficult. However, with practice and detachment, it can be mastered."

A conquered mind does not mean a dull and dead person. On the contrary, it means a sharp and alert intellect. In other words, while the mind is made silent, the intellect remains alert and aware. This alert intellect with a calm mind is the very essence of Ananda.

It was the last of the 21 days of the COVID lockdown. Virat and Varsha were happy that they would now be able to

move out of the house, albeit with some restrictions. On the other hand, both Priya and Rajan were pleased that the 'work from home' arrangement was going to continue too, at least for a few more weeks.

Three weeks of lockdown had also meant considerably more family time, which in turn had resulted in better bonding between the four members of the Rajan family. All four were enjoying having their tea and meals together every day, joint watching of TV shows, as well as their joint conversations, most of which had been about Rajan's notes on Sanatana Dharma.

Today, Virat and Varsha had made the tea and some bhel puri to go with it. There was a happy vibe in the Rajan household.

"While Psychiatry and Psychoanalysis are just about a century old in modern science, our scriptures seem to have understood thousands of years ago that mental health is critical for a person's overall well-being. I find that truly remarkable," said Rajan starting off the discussion. "It is only today that medical science says that a majority of diseases are psychosomatic i.e. caused by the mind."

"As opposed to this, the ancient Sanatan Dharma philosophy is predominantly about managing and controlling the mind," added Rajan. "That," he emphasised, "is the key to our success and happiness."

"*I see that both you and Amma have been doing meditation every morning for two or three years now. What changes have you felt in yourselves?*" *asked Varsha.*

"For starters, we fight much less now. We are less possessive about our views and are more open to letting go if it can stop a conversation from blowing up into a fight. We listen better to each other now." Priya was clearly benefiting.

"Amma is better than me, and I still have a distance to cover before I can be as giving. Maybe that has also to do with the fact that she is far more regular in her meditation than I am. While I often miss my meditation on Sundays and holidays, Amma simply does not," said Rajan in admiration.

"To answer your question specifically, I feel I have benefited hugely through my meditation. I am calmer within myself, much happier in general, and much less bitter about the world. I would go as far as to say that meditation has transformed me," added Rajan. Priya nodded in agreement.

"I too am beginning to notice some of the changes. The way we have handled these discussions among us, without turning them into bitter arguments, is a good indicator of your transformation," said Virat in corroboration.

"I have tried to meditate occasionally, but every time I found it almost impossible to stay focused on any one object even for a few minutes. So I gave up," said Varsha recounting her experience.

"A common mistake that most beginners make in meditation is obsessing about getting it absolutely right and achieving complete mental silence, or experiencing something extraordinary. This could result in demotivation and also in eventually giving it up. The most important thing is to just stick to the process and keep at it. Like most things in life, in meditation too one gets better and better with practice," explained Rajan.

"There will be good days and bad days in meditation. One should not be affected by a bad day when the mind wanders away too many times. Even if you are able to 'catch' your mind wandering repeatedly during your meditation and keep 'bringing it back' again and again, it is a very beneficial practice and helps develop skills in witnessing the mind. In the worst scenario, even if it amounts to merely sitting still at one place for some time, it could still help in reducing the stress of a restless and anxious person." Rajan's keenness that his children started working on their minds with some regular practice was evident.

"There are so many schools of meditation. How can one choose among them?" *Virat was beginning to show some intent now.*

"I suggest you keep it simple to start with. Sit in a comfortable position in a dark room with eyes closed. Breathe slowly and focus on your breath, pausing for a second between your inhale and exhale. Continue for 15 minutes at least. Try and do that for six months, and you will get into some rhythm and definitely start experiencing some benefits. You can then experiment with more techniques advocated by different schools, and see what works best for you. I experimented too, only to realise that the simple technique I described works best for me. It works for Amma too."

"I am keen that the two of you start devoting some time every day to work on your mind, just as you do daily workouts for your body. The next twenty odd years might be the most challenging for you, both in your personal and professional lives. Working on your mind right from now will help you navigate these challenges successfully. You will make fewer mistakes, both in your interactions with people and in your decision-making. I find it rather ironic that people start meditating after their retirement, and not during their youth and middle age, when their mind was coping with the toughest challenges of their lives." Rajan was speaking from experience.

"Did you practise meditation and Sakshi Bhava when you were our age?" asked Varsha.

"That is my single biggest regret with respect to my professional career. Life presented me with some wonderful opportunities to surge ahead in my career. However, I blew them purely because of poor mind management. In my mid-30s, I was the de facto CEO of an MNC that I had helped set up shop in India. My boss was a 60-year-old European who was happy to lead an easy and relaxed life and let me run the show. I worked very hard and delivered some great results. I am sure that if I had just hung in there for another year or two, I would have been formally named the CEO of the company's India operations. However, I could not handle the work-induced stress, and this impacted my dealings with my boss and other colleagues. I allowed my ego to get the better of me repeatedly and ended up picking too many fights. In the process, I pushed myself into a corner from where resigning from my job was the only way to my peace. Today, it is one of the most respected organisations in the world."

"Looking back, I am absolutely sure that had I practised meditation and Sakshi Bhava during those days, I would have handled my challenges much better and come out victorious. And today, I could well have been sitting on the global board of that organisation, delivering a much wider impact through my work."

"And what about Pranayama? Would you recommend I do Pranayama too?" *asked Varsha.*

"Considering how often you are affected by nasal allergies, I would most certainly recommend it for you," Priya's response was spontaneous.

"However, that would be the smaller benefit. The primary benefit of Pranayama is how well it prepares me for meditation. Every day, I do Pranayama for five minutes before commencing my meditation."

"The Pranayama I do is called Anulom-Vilom Pranayama. It basically involves slow and long breathing in a rhythm. I inhale through my right nostril for eight counts, hold the breath for four counts, and then exhale through the left nostril for twelve counts. I then repeat the same, this time inhaling through the left nostril, holding, and exhaling through the right. I repeat this for five minutes using a timer before starting my meditation. And it helps. The odd occasion when I skip this part, my meditation experience falls a little short," added Priya.

"Witnessing your own mind in action. That is so fascinating. Have you ever tried doing it, Appa?" *There was genuine curiosity in Virat's voice.*

"Only over the last couple of years," responded Rajan with a smile. "I have managed to do it even in the middle

of some difficult conversations, checking what was going on in my mind, and how I was feeling, thinking, reacting, and responding. That was very helpful. I could stop myself from making some blunders in those critical conversations, only because I was watching my mind. I am clear that it can greatly help me in my interactions with people. It also helps me understand myself and my typical failings that are driven by my innate nature, so much better. It is yet to become a habit though. I simply forget to witness my mind quite often. However, I am totally convinced about its value in our lives."

Section D

Frequently Discussed Topics

This section covers the topics that get discussed perhaps the most in living rooms and social media. These include the aspects of Hinduism that are most visible, like caste and rituals, which often come under attack by its critics and detractors. Also included in this section are topics that are most abstract like 'Advaita' and Detachment. People generally tend to have questions on these topics.

Chapters in this Section

Chapter 19

Varna and Caste

The caste system of today is the result of gross misuse and misinterpretation of the ancient varna system over centuries by vested interests!

The ancient Hindu society consisted of four broad social groups or varnas based on their skills and profession. These were the Brahmins (the priests), the Kshatriyas (the warriors and soldiers), the Vaishyas (traders and businessmen), and Shudras (the workers and labourers). This does not seem to be much different from what was prevalent in almost all societies even during the Middle Ages. The societies in the West too had the kings and nobles as the ruling class, the priestly class as the authority on all religious matters, the businessmen to keep the economy running, and the labour class for doing the actual manual work.

As opposed to what it has become now, there are grounds to believe that in ancient Bharat, the Varna (now loosely referred to as caste) which corresponded to a person's occupation, was not determined based on birth, but on his skills and Prakriti. It also appears that there was no hierarchy between the different castes. No caste was seen as superior or inferior to the other. The following verses from the Bhagavad Gita are relevant in this context:

Chapter IV, verse 13:

चातुर्वर्ण्यं मया सृष्टं गुणकर्मविभागश:।
तस्य कर्तारमपि मां विद्ध्यकर्तारमव्ययम्॥

Chātur-varṇyaṁ mayā sṛiṣhṭaṁ guṇa-karma-vibhāgaśhaḥ
tasya kartāram api māṁ viddhyakartāram avyayam

Translation

"The fourfold caste has been created by Me according to the differentiation of GUNA and KARMA; though I am the author thereof, know Me as non-doer and immutable." [The Holy Geeta, Commentary by Swami Chinmayananda][14]

People become suited to one of the four varnas because of their Gunas that constitute their innate nature, which in turn is shaped by their Karma over

---

14 From Swami Chinmayananda's commentary on the Bhagavad Gita in a book titled "The Holy Geeta"

all their lives. While God is the creator of this scheme, he is not responsible for anyone's individual Karma, which is always determined by that person's free will.

Chapter XVIII, verse 41

ब्राह्मणक्षत्रियविशां शूद्राणां च परन्तप।
कर्माणि प्रविभक्तानि स्वभावप्रभवैर्गुणै:॥

brāhmaṇa-kṣhatriya-viśhāṁ śhūdrāṇāṁ cha parantapa
karmāṇi pravibhaktāni svabhāva-prabhavair guṇaiḥ

Translation

"Of scholars (BRAHMANAS), of leaders (KSHATRIYAS), and of traders (VAISYAS), as well as of workers (SUDRAS), O Parantapa, the duties are distributed according to the qualities born of their nature." [The Holy Geeta, Commentary by Swami Chinmayananda][15]

A person's work is determined according to the person's qualities which emanate from their Prakriti or innate nature. This verse is a clear assertion that a person's varna or caste is not based on the person's birth.

---

15 From Swami Chinmayananda's commentary on the Bhagavad Gita in a book titled "The Holy Geeta"

Chapter V, verse 18:

विद्याविनयसम्पन्ने ब्राह्मणे गवि हस्तिनि।
शुनि चैव श्वपाके च पण्डिता: समदर्शिन:॥

vidyā-vinaya-sampanne brāhmaṇe gavi hastini
śhuni chaiva śhva-pāke cha paṇḍitāḥ sama-darśhinaḥ

Translation

"Sages look with an equal eye upon a BRAHMANA endowed with learning and humility, upon a cow, upon an elephant, and even upon a dog and an outcast." [The Holy Geeta, Commentary by Swami Chinmayananda][16]

Wise men do not ever discriminate between living beings - be it a learned Brahmin, an animal, or a person with no social status.

Some more quotes on Varna (caste) from our scriptures:

- If one shows the symptoms of being a Brahmana, Kshatriya, Vaishya or Shudra as described above, even if he has appeared in a different caste, he should be accepted according to those symptoms of classification. (Srimad Bhagavatam 7.11.35)

- Not **birth,** nor samskaras, nor study of the Vedas, nor ancestry are the causes of being a Brahman.

---

16 From Swami Chinmayananda's commentary on the Bhagavad Gita in a book titled "The Holy Geeta"

Conduct alone is the cause [Mahabharata Anushasana Parva 143:50]

In reality, though, things have not panned out as envisaged above. Over time, this system of division of society based on occupation got severely distorted. Vested interests among some castes misinterpreted and twisted the original intention of the Varna system and abused it to exploit and discriminate against people of other castes over centuries. This has made caste the bane of Hindu society today.

These vested interests have exerted their privileges fully but not discharged their duties. They have also made their caste a birthright for successive generations in their families, irrespective of merit or suitability. India's democratically elected governments have enacted laws and taken several measures to address this societal ill. Societal reforms too are happening, albeit slowly. These require more intensity and more widespread support, not just in letter but in spirit as well.

It was 20 years since Devki had started working as a maid in the Rajan household. Devki lost her husband early and had to bring up her two daughters, Sailaja and Supriya, on her own. During their childhood, Sailaja and Supriya would often accompany their mother to Rajan's house. The

strong bond of love and friendship between Devki and her two daughters was always heartwarming to see. Devki had great work ethics too and was excellent in her work. No wonder she and her two daughters were treated by the Rajan family as their own. The Rajans had also financially assisted the education of Sailaja and Supriya.

Just a year ago, the Rajans heard that Sailaja had eloped with a young man from another caste, despite opposition to the relationship from Devki. Since then, Devki had to literally disown her, as otherwise she risked being ostracised by her own community. Devki feared that this, in turn, might make it very difficult for her to find a suitable match from within her community for her second daughter, Supriya. Needless to say, a pall of gloom had descended on the lives of Devki and her daughters, and the Rajans felt helpless that they could do little to help. Devki, in particular, was devastated by this forced separation from Sailaja.

The Rajans, therefore, had some first-hand experience of the havoc that caste could cause in people's lives.

"We have to unanimously agree that the caste system is totally unacceptable, Appa. How can we discriminate against someone based on their birth, in today's age?" Virat's strong views on the matter could hardly wait to erupt.

"I can't agree more with you, Virat. Whatever might have been the intent behind the original Varna system, *today it is well and truly past its 'use by' date," agreed Rajan.*

"If so, why does the Hindu community not speak in one voice and put an end to it? Looks like not all Hindus think like you even today." *Virat was persistent with expressing his genuine agony.*

"You are right again. However, many Hindus are standing up against the caste system too, and that number is growing," said Rajan, adding, "Post-independence, despite an 80% plus Hindu population, India has enacted laws making caste-based discrimination illegal. Several other affirmative government actions have been taken, like reservations for lower castes in higher education and government jobs, in order to reduce the inequalities in society. And there are several social organisations that actively fight against caste-based discrimination," said Rajan.

"And if you look at upper middle class families in metro cities, caste is a non-issue amongst the youth today," added Priya.

"Are you both suggesting that enough has been done already?" *Virat was in no mood to let this discussion end soon.*

"Not at all," admitted Rajan. "Progress is much slower than what might be desired. Governments can only

do so much. Rapid voluntary reforms within society are the need of the hour. The politics around caste too are not making these reforms any easier since the very survival of certain political parties and politicians depends on perpetuating the feeling of victimhood and exploitation."

"Despite these challenges, there is steady forward movement, albeit slow."

"My friend's parents have told her sister clearly that if she decides to marry outside their caste, they would not participate in the wedding. Is that not unhealthy pressure? Finding a good partner for yourself is so difficult. On top of that, if so many conditions are imposed, it is so unfair." Varsha was lamenting the needless challenges her friend's sister was being put through.

"But then inter-caste marriages have increased these days, and also there is increased acceptance of such marriages. In our own wider family, quite a few inter-caste marriages have happened over the last five years," pitched in Priya.

"That is not happening in all sections of society and across all geographies within India. It may be limited to certain sections of the upper middle class in metro cities," added Rajan.

"What about our priests? Can non-Brahmins become priests in Hinduism?" *asked Virat.*

"There are several temples in India today with non-Brahmin priests, including several with Dalit priests. However, I would imagine that most temples still have only Brahmins as priests. We should also understand that there would be many more layers and nuances that might need to be factored into these discussions, and that we may not know enough."

"That said, the four of us would definitely like to see a Hindu society free of discrimination, and so would many of our Hindu friends and relatives. While reforms are happening, we agree that a lot more needs to be done, and at a much faster pace."

"In summary, I see caste-based discrimination as an aberration within the wider philosophy of Hinduism, which undoubtedly needs to be addressed through reforms. However, it would be both unfair and foolish to discard the entire philosophy because of this one aspect," *said Rajan.*

"Incidentally, I have told Devki that she can meet Sailaja and her husband in our house, away from the gaze of her community, anytime. She is very happy and said she will do so soon," *announced Priya, to everyone's delight.*

Chapter 20

Ritualistic Prayers and Practises

To judge every Hindu ritual or practice by merely what meets an uninformed eye would amount to missing the woods for the trees!

For most Hindus, the worshipping of forms, the chanting of mantras, visiting temples, and complying with rituals help. They help overcome fears and insecurities and bring about a certain mental integration. The same applies to big religious events where a large number of people come together to express and celebrate their common beliefs. All such actions have the ability to provide peace and security, besides getting people into a frame of mind suited for a spiritual pursuit. In the case of most people, these are necessary aids to focus on God and to reach a higher plane of realisation and awareness.

One need not be shy of trying to relate to a Personal God (like Krishna, Shiva, Ganesha, Hanuman) or to participate in pujas to inculcate and nurture a feeling of pure love and Bhakti. This could purify one's heart and get one into a better mental space for higher pursuits and experiences. Japas and Mantras can also be tools to prepare your mind for meditation or for meditation itself. Swami Chinmayananda in his book Kindle Life says:

"The technique of japa and mantra lies in engaging the mind totally in a self-repeated sound, having a very subtle and a great philosophical significance, and after a time when the mind is fully engrossed with the idea, we cry a halt to it, thereby taking away from the mind its only occupation at that time. The hope of the scriptures is that by such a process the seeker would come to experience the silence of the heart (mind)"[17]

The mantras often have a highly uplifting meaning and impact. The famous Gayatri Mantra and its meaning are as follows:

ॐ भूर्भुवः स्वः तत्सवितुर्वरेण्यं भर्गो देवस्य धीमहि धियो यो नः प्रचोदयात् ॥

Om Bhurbhuah suvaha tatsaviturvarenyam
bhargodevasya dheemahi dhiyoyonah prachodayaat

---

17 From Swami Chinmayananda's book 'Kindle Life'

Translated by Swami Chinmayananda in his book Kindle Life as "May my intellect be steady without agitation; may it be clean without the dirt of passions, may the light of consciousness come to shine forth a brilliant beam of its radiance through my intellect." In other words, "May my perception of the world be clearer, my discrimination subtler, and my judgements correct and quick, my comprehension of situations and beings precise and wise."[18]

---

18 From Swami Chinmayananda's book 'Kindle Life'

"I am unable to relate to our rituals and pujas. The priest chants something in Sanskrit which even he himself might not understand. And while he is chanting, often people are not even listening to him, but doing their own thing," *Virat's observations were not entirely incorrect.*

"It is fine if you do not like participating in our pujas. However, you do not have to announce it from the rooftops and make a spectacle out of it. If we have a puja in the house where all our relatives have been invited, merely being present does not mean you endorse every ritual in that puja." *Priya was clearly still carrying the hurt of Virat's deliberate absence on the day they had conducted the puja with the extended family.*

> *"A part of the chaos we see in some of our religious gatherings is also because of the fact that there are no strict do's and don'ts in Hinduism," clarified Rajan.*

> *"You go to any neighbourhood temple, and you will see each individual doing his own thing. Someone is chanting shlokas, someone else is prostrating on the floor in front of the deity, a third one is walking around the deity, while a fourth is sitting down with his eyes closed in meditation even in the middle of all this. While on one hand it results in a more chaotic atmosphere, on the other hand it also shows the absence of strict rules," said Rajan making a virtue out of the chaos one might see in some temples.*

"And why do Hindus chant so many mantras which they do not understand? How could that possibly benefit anyone? I find little sense in most of what we do in the name of religion," *Varsha was in an unsparing mood.*

"Incidentally, it has been established that repetitive and rhythmic chanting of mantras has a calming effect on the human mind."

"Worshipping various forms of God, chanting mantras, visiting temples and complying with rituals might appear meaningless to you, but they do give millions of people a feeling of security, happiness and peace."

"These can also help to get us into the right frame of mind for seeking and experiencing union with God. In the case of many people, these practises are hugely helpful to focus on God, get into a zone within their mind, and then to progressively reach a higher spiritual plane," Rajan's comments were not without merit.

"The broader question here is probably not just why chant, but why do we have so many different mantras / chants? Can't they all be the same humming if the answer is built around a 'feeling of comfort'?" *asked a persistent Virat.*

"These mantras carry messages that are meant to motivate and inspire people to stay on the right path. They were composed by Sanskrit speakers and were

obviously understood by several generations that followed. For them, it was not the chanting alone but also the accompanying messages that mattered. Successive generations memorised them just by virtue of hearing them over and over again. People who chant them today without fully grasping their meaning still recognise that they carry important messages or praise for God, and this gives them a feeling of fulfilment," explained Rajan.

"But then what is the logic behind offering food and clothes to idols, or to bathe them in milk? Is that not a colossal wastage of resources? And I detest this concept of offering money to God, or 'striking a deal' with God that if my wishes are fulfilled, I shall 'gift' something to God in return. Are our Gods corruptible?" *Virat was emphatic about his disapproval of these practises.*

"I am not going to try to defend every religious practice or ritual within Hinduism. Some of the practises would appear to be unwarranted to a purely logical mind. But then let us remember, down the ages, men have made them what they are today, through various interpretations of our philosophy, some of them flawed. I am reminded of what Kofi Annan, a former UN Secretary-General, had once very famously said. He had said something to the effect that the problem is never with the faith, but with the faithful. I agree that several

flawed practises that have crept into Hinduism might need reform.

"That said, let us also examine the broad concept of offering food, clothes, and gifts to God from the point of view of Bhakti Yoga or the path of love. Don't we all feel that a mother's love for her child is arguably the purest form of love? And how does the mother express her love for her child? By bathing, dressing, feeding the child, and so forth. Therefore, it is important to understand the spirit behind several of these practises and not focus solely on the act and describe it as foolish or akin to corruption.

"And the money that devotees offer in temples is not wasted. It gets used primarily for the subsistence of the people working in the temple and for meeting the temple's expenses. In several famous temples which receive large sums as offerings, a substantial part gets spent on public welfare. The administration of many of these big temples is in the hands of the government.

"In many temples, the food offerings to the God get distributed to the devotees and the poor who gather outside these temples. There is still some wastage. However, in my personal opinion, given the solace which these practises bring to millions, it might not be such a huge price to pay."

"*And finally, it is also important to remember in this context that nobody is ever compelled to follow anything in Hinduism,*" said Rajan, presenting what could be described as a believer's perspective.

"If nobody is ever compelled, why were you and Amma upset at my not being present for our puja?" countered Virat.

"*Being upset is different from compelling someone to comply with rituals. The fact that you did not attend the puja shows that you were not compelled. Secondly, you knew how important the puja was for us and how hard we had worked to organise it. Your decision to skip the event put us in a spot in front of our relatives and was insensitive,*" responded a slightly emotional Priya.

"Amma and Appa, both of you do daily prayers in our puja room. How does it help you?" asked Varsha, quickly changing the direction of the discussion.

"*Oh, it helps me a lot. It gives me a feeling of security and peace. My prayers are an acceptance that there is so much in my life over which I have no control. That helps me shed my ego and makes me more humble.*"

"*I also love listening to several of our Sanskrit shlokas. I often find great solace while listening to them,*" said Priya.

Rajan's views on prayers were a surprise to the other three. "My time in the puja room helps me in a number of ways. I chant shlokas, mostly within my mind, and that improves my concentration. After the shlokas, I pray to my Personal Gods to help me think right. After all, our thoughts are the source of all our words and actions.

"Since I believe in the Karma theory, I know that prayers cannot change my fate or my Prarabdha Karma playing out its predetermined course. All I can do is focus on my current Karma and get them right. That alone can help me overcome the challenges that might come my way and improve both my present and future. Therefore, I seek the Almighty's blessings to be able to exercise my free will or Purushartha wisely and effectively every time.

"Prayers also provide me with the confidence to take the risks that one must to make a bigger impact in, and get more out of, life. Without prayers, I might not have been able to muster the confidence to give up working in the corporate world and pursue social work and hobbies instead."

"And once I am done with my prayers, I focus on the face of my Personal God, Vishnu, for about ten minutes, while keeping my mind as thought-free as possible. I feel good doing that. It centres my mind before starting off

on my work for the day. That is how I use my time in the puja room."

"I have never been able to understand the significance of the religious rituals during our weddings. Less than a fourth of the guests show any interest in the rituals. Most of the guests end up forming small groups and keep chatting amongst themselves, while the priest continues the pujas with the couple, for hours." *Virat's observations were not entirely incorrect.*

"Amma, can you explain some of the important elements in our wedding rituals and their significance?" *asked a curious Varsha.*

"The rituals vary between different social groups within the Hindu community, while also being similar in several parts," said Priya. "I can tell you about some of the key rituals followed in our families.

"A fun part is when the boy and the girl exchange garlands as their relatives lift them up, making it a challenge for the couple to land the garland correctly around each other's neck. This adds festivity to the occasion."

*"Then you have the **Kanyadanam** where the father places his daughter's hands in the hands of the groom, symbolising his wholehearted consent to the wedding and also the girl's transition from being a daughter to a*

wife, while imploring the groom to accept his daughter as his equal partner at all times."

"This is followed by **Mangalya Dharanam**, where the bride sits on her father's lap while the groom ties the mangalsutra around her neck as a symbol of his commitment to everlasting love, friendship, and companionship."

"Then we have the **Saptapadi** or the seven steps, where holding the bride's hand and feet, the groom walks seven steps with her, symbolising seven vows. I had memorised these vows before my marriage. The seven vows are:

> Step 1: To respect and honour each other. With the first step, we seek the Lord's blessings and commit to nourishing each other's lives, meeting each other's needs and enriching our journey together, forever.

> Step 2: To offer each other the unwavering physical, mental, and spiritual support needed to lead healthy, happy, and fulfilling lives

> Step 3: To be faithful to each other and endeavour to construct a life of wealth, wisdom, and prosperity for ourselves and our children

> Step 4: To fulfil the physical needs of each other and stand by each other through all the difficult times. To be ever grateful for the happiness that we provide to each other.

Step 5: To beget and raise virtuous and noble children. To always be aware of our responsibility towards all living creatures and the universe.

Step 6: To age together, fighting sickness and celebrating health. To lead long, peaceful, and prosperous lives.

Step 7: To live a life of friendship, love, and mutual trust

After these seven steps, the couple accept each other as husband and wife and enter into the eternal commitment called marriage."

"You may call me old-fashioned or a die-hard romantic, for I fell in love with these vows the first time I heard them. In North India, instead of the Saptapadi, you have the ritual of saat pheres where the couple walk around the sacred fire seven times." Priya's detailed answer was filled with a positive emotion, as though she was reliving her own marriage.

"Wow! This is what today's commitment-phobic generation needs badly," *said a thoroughly impressed Varsha.*

"You do not need the rituals to convey your commitment to your partner," *countered Virat.*

"Do not see these solely as religious rituals. They also represent our traditions and culture, and give us our

distinct identity," said Rajan, looking at Virat to see if he was anywhere close to changing his stand on not having a traditional wedding. Virat's silence did not reveal his mind.

Chapter 21

Detachment

No, Hinduism does not mandate that you should have no desires!

One common apprehension most people have about Sanatana Dharma or Hinduism is that it may require one to give up all of one's desires and live a life of absolute abstinence and renunciation. This is not true. Sanatana Dharma recognises both the need and significance of desire and gives it the status of power (Shakti) through the concept of **Ichcha Shakti** or the Power of Desire. Unless you want to achieve something strongly enough, your resolve to achieve it cannot be strong, which in turn will affect your chances of success.

There is an inherent contradiction in telling a man seeking Ananda to give up all desires. Isn't the desire for Ananda itself a desire? That said, as one progresses in one's spiritual path, the nature of one's desires changes and evolves. As a teenager who is very passionate about playing cricket, you might have felt very possessive about your cricket bat. When you are 50, you may still like the old cricket bat as it kindles happy memories of your childhood and may even use it occasionally to play with your son. However, you would certainly not feel possessive about it. What changed, and how? A degree of detachment has automatically come about within you towards the cricket bat, just by virtue of your growing up and evolving. This is the type of detachment, i.e., 'love without possessiveness', that is prescribed by our scriptures.

Obsessive attachment to anything leading to possessiveness is binding and works against our freedom. When we acquire something as our possession driven by intense desire, we may feel we have gained control over it. However, often it is the possession that controls us. For instance, sometimes you might have seen a person walking around with a big and aggressive pet on a leash, struggling to control it. While the leash ensures that the pet cannot leave its owner, it also ensures the owner cannot leave the pet. Similarly, we have often seen people feeling compelled to remain close to their prized possessions for fear of losing them, surrendering a part of their freedom in the process. Therefore, often our possessions too possess us.

There is also a fundamental difference between obsessive attachment and true love. In fact, attachment leading to possessiveness is the exact opposite of love. Such attachment to anyone or anything automatically distances us from all else. Our family should not become the endpoint of our love or the object of our exclusive attachment. It should, in fact, become the starting point for our love, from where it spreads far and wide.

Our scriptures are pragmatic. They do not ask us to run away from the material world and lead the life of an ascetic in order to attain Ananda. They say we can do it right where we are, continuing to pursue our professional, personal, and family life. All we need is to balance between the following four goals of human life:

- Dharma **or Duties** - Each one of us has certain duties. Providing one's family with food, shelter, clothing, necessary comforts, and protection is a primary duty.

- Artha **or Wealth** - Our scriptures recognise wealth as an important human need. Earning enough money to provide ourselves and our family a life of dignity is very important. Wealth creation is a legitimate activity so long as it is done by rightful means and not by depriving others of their share, and as long as the wealth is not applied for wrong ends or left behind in the wrong hands.

- Kama **or Desire for Sensory Pleasures** is not forbidden either. The Bhagavad Gita merely sounds a note of caution. Pursue sensory pleasures, but in moderation. Take care not to end up as a slave to your senses. If you exercise such moderation, you shall have far greater control over your destiny.

* Moksha **or liberation from the cycle of life and death** through one or more of the four paths of Karma Yoga, Jnana Yoga, Bhakti Yoga, and Raja Yoga. As we have said earlier, none of these paths require one to become an ascetic. They need sustained work on oneself, particularly one's mind, which can be done even by people engaged in worldly pursuits.

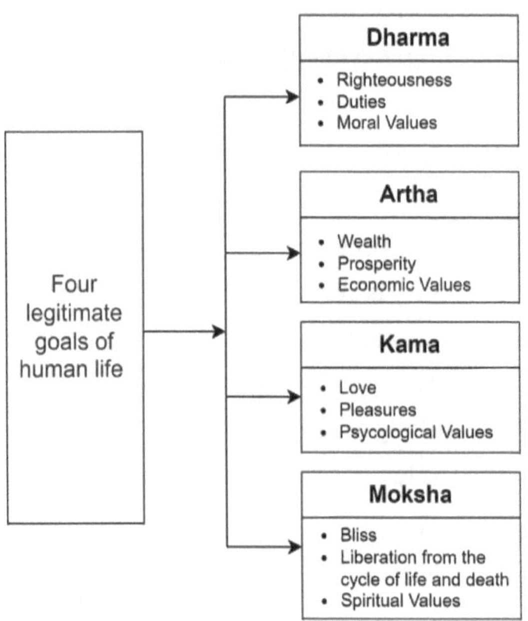

According to the Bhagavad Gita, a householder's life is no less noble or challenging than that of an ascetic who spends all his time meditating in isolation. Pursuit of desires is legitimate, so long as one does not become a slave to such pursuit. The following verses from the Bhagavad Gita speak about the need to exercise moderation in the pursuit of physical pleasures:

Chapter VI, verse 16

नात्यश्नतस्तु योगोऽस्ति न चैकान्तमनश्नतः|
न चाति स्वप्नशीलस्य जाग्रतो नैव चार्जुन||

nātyaśhnatastu yogo 'sti na chaikāntam anaśhnataḥ
na chāti-svapna-śhīlasya jāgrato naiva chārjuna

Translation

"Verily, YOGA is not possible for him who eats too much, nor for him who does not eat at all; nor for him who sleeps too much, nor for him who is (always) awake, O Arjuna." [The Holy Geeta, Commentary by Swami Chinmayananda][19]

Our scriptures do not recommend that we ignore our body while pursuing spiritual growth. Food and sleep are key for a healthy body. However, moderation with respect to both is recommended.

---

19 From Swami Chinmayananda's commentary on the Bhagavad Gita, in a book titled "The Holy Geeta"

Chapter VI, verse 17

युक्ताहारविहारस्य युक्तचेष्टस्य कर्मसु।
युक्तस्वप्नावबोधस्य योगो भवति दुःखहा॥

yuktāhāra-vihārasya yukta-cheshṭasya karmasu

yukta-svapnāvabodhasya yogo bhavati duḥkha-hā

Translation

"Yoga becomes the destroyer of pain for him who is moderate in eating and recreation, who is moderate in his exertion during his actions, who is moderate in sleep and wakefulness." [The Holy Geeta, Commentary by Swami Chinmayananda][20]

Yoga is most effective in its stated objective of helping a person attain Ananda when the person practises moderation with respect to the pursuit and enjoyment of physical pleasures.

In summary, Sanatana Dharma recommends:

- 'true and expansive love' - and not - 'attachment and possessiveness'

- 'Desire with moderation' - and not - 'obsession'.

---

20 From Swami Chinmayananda's commentary on the Bhagavad Gita, in a book titled "The Holy Geeta"

It was December, and the season of date palm jaggery in Kolkata. The Bengalis call this jaggery 'Patali Gur' or 'Nolen Gur' (the latter being the name for the liquid variant of the jaggery). Sweets made using Nolen Gur instead of white sugar, like Gurer Sondesh and Gurer Roshogolla, are some of the most delicious things you can eat anywhere in the world.

Rajan still had several childhood friends in Kolkata, all of whom knew the Rajan family's weakness for sweets. It was customary for the family to get supplies of delicious Bengali sweets made with palm jaggery every winter. This December was no exception.

The latest supply to arrive consisted of two boxes of Gurer Sondesh and a bottle of Nolen Gur. Both were disappearing fast because Rajan loved having the Nolen Gur as a dessert by itself.

'Pure heaven,' exclaimed Priya as she bit into yet another Sondesh. 'All healthy diet plans have been put on hold until these sweets last.'

"But remember, you need to give up these temptations, if you wish to grow spiritually and attain Ananda," Varsha's comment drew peals of laughter from the other three. Gradually, the discussions around desire and renunciation grew more serious.

"Numerous Hindu gurus and saints say that desire is the root cause of all misery, and giving up all desires is the only way to salvation or liberation. However, I find that to be against the very spirit of human life and existence, and extremely demotivating." *Priya clearly had not found merit in such advice. Her comment found immediate agreement with both Virat and Varsha.*

"Such extreme interpretation is bound to demotivate. That is why the Bhagavad Gita stepped in to clarify that what is required is moderation. Enjoying good food is fine, but do not overindulge and spoil your health. Earn money for a comfortable life without allowing money to become the sole purpose of your life. That would amount to confusing the means (wealth) to be the end (happiness)."

"Love by all means, but without turning possessive. Else you are bound to hurt yourself as well as the object of such possessive love," explained Rajan.

"Excessive desires that take the shape of obsession will enslave you to these objects of desire. Even when they get satisfied, such excessive desires can only result in greed for more. And when not satisfied, they result in frustration and anger."

"Remember at all times that the real and lasting source of sustained happiness lies within you and not outside. It depends on how you manage your mind using your

intellect. This requires you to look within and work on yourself. Obsessive pursuit of external material desires will distract you from this path. That is why our scriptures prescribe moderation in the pursuit of such desires and pleasures."

"Don't you think this concept of detachment if internalised would rob you of all passion. Can a detached person be passionate about achieving anything big in life? Could Steve Jobs have achieved whatever he did if he was detached?" *As a young man seeking to achieve success in his career and life, Virat's concern was perfectly understandable.*

"Steve Jobs's journey had several ups and downs. He could not have achieved what he did if he had allowed the first major setback itself to push him into a depressed and defeatist mindset. If you want to be an achiever over an extended period of time, you cannot get too attached to any short-term goal or outcome, to the extent that it becomes an obsession. Detachment, the way it has been imagined in Sanatana Dharma, does not mean disinterest leading to lesser energy. On the contrary, such detachment will help you stay the course, by giving you immunity from short-term setbacks and failures. This would be clear if you study the life of anybody who has achieved great results over a long span of time, be it Nelson Mandela or Mahatma Gandhi or a sports person like Mary Kom.

In other words, such detachment will help you overcome excessive fears, anxieties, and insecurities. And when you rise above fear, anxiety and insecurity, your ability to engage with life improves drastically. You can tackle any challenge without the fear of failure, humiliation, or embarrassment. These limitations, which generally hold back people from giving their best, will cease to exist!" Rajan's explanation made a lot of sense.

"How do we determine what moderation is?" *questioned Varsha.*

"When deciding what separates moderation from excess, we should consider the consequences of our actions. If we weigh both the pleasure and the outcomes honestly, the overall result will guide us in knowing whether to proceed or not. The key is to be truthful when balancing the value of the pleasure against the impact of the consequences," explained Rajan.

"Can I have one more Sondesh, please?" Virat's question suggested that all attempts at moderation would have to wait for a few more days.

Chapter 22

Advaita, Dvaita and Vishishtadvaita

If God is everywhere and in everything, how can you and I be different from God?

Post the beginning of the common era, Hinduism's survival was threatened by the very religious tolerance and diversity of thoughts that it allowed. A number of new religions like Buddhism and Jainism had taken firm roots. The continued abuse of the caste system by vested interests within the Hindus was also inducing some people to seek alternatives.

It was under these circumstances, around the 8th century CE, that Hinduism produced a towering intellectual and genius, Shankara, who almost single-handedly rescued Hinduism through his brilliant interpretation of the Upanishadic philosophy called **'Advaita'**.

Adi Shankara

In a brief lifespan of a mere 32 years, Shankara mastered the scriptures, wrote extensively and exquisitely, traversed the length and breadth of the country propounding his signature Advaita philosophy and winning over almost the entire spiritual intelligentsia of the land through debates and discourses. He also set up four mutts (monasteries) in the four corners of the country. How he managed to do all this in the 8th century, overcoming all the unimaginable challenges of terrain and language, and within such a short lifespan, is beyond comprehension. No wonder most Hindus regard him not just as another human being, but as an avatar of Lord Shiva.

The Advaita concept was not invented by Shankara, but he is the one who propounded it to such an extent that today it has become arguably the most defining aspect of Hindu spiritual thought. The word Advaita means non-duality or **Monism**. According to Shankara's Advaita, there is no difference between man and God, and everyone and everything is a manifestation of the same God and Godliness.

According to the Advaita philosophy, anything finite including man can never be separate from the infinite, i.e. God. Therefore, in reality, man has no distinct identity outside the identity of God. Take, for instance, a wave. Once a wave subsides, the wave's water is still there in the sea, though the wave itself (in its name and form) ceases to exist. Take off the name and form from anything, and the essence that remains is God. God is the reality in everything.

In essence, the Advaita theory says that there is no question of anything other than God being in existence, since God is everywhere and in everything. We see millions of forms around us as different and distinct from each other because of our ignorance of our real Self, our Atman, which is nothing but God inside us. It is this ignorance or Maya that causes the illusion of a manifold world with endless differences. Once we, through the right knowledge and efforts, experience the God inside us and in everything around us, we see the whole universe as just one undivided existence.

Therefore, as per the Advaita philosophy, there is no question of saying 'God and I'. There is only God. So long as we see ourselves as different from God, we continue to feel afraid and insecure. However, once we know our real self to be God; what can we be afraid of? So long as we see the world as full of distinct and separate entities, fear and insecurity remain. It is only when we do not see or feel the presence of anyone other than ourselves, and see ourselves as one with the entire universe, that our fear ceases to exist.

There is no point in running all around the world in search of happiness. God, the ultimate happiness or Ananda, is already within us. This has merely got shrouded in Maya. We need to unravel, understand, and perceive this fully. The essence of Advaita is 'believe in yourself first, and then believe in anything else', since the ultimate power is already within. This reality is beyond the reach of intellectual comprehension. It can only be experienced. Feeling the oneness with God internally is most difficult. It comes after years (or lives) of sadhana or intense effort. This is the doctrine of Advaita in a nutshell.

Ramanujacharya (11th century CE) and Madhavacharya (12th century CE), two great Hindu gurus who came after Shankara, disagreed with him. Ramanujacharya's interpretation, known as **Vishishtadvaita** (Qualified Monism), says that while man and God are not the same, man is a part or aspect of God. Therefore, every man has the potential to attain God, blessed as he is with the same divine essence. Vishishtadvaita does, however, accept the traditional Vedanta position of salvation through the merger of Atman with Paramatma.

Madhavacharya's **Dvaita** (Dualism) philosophy goes one step further in drawing a clear difference between man and God. It says that man and God are entirely different and distinct entities. The two can never merge, though man can get liberated from the cycle of births and deaths through devotion to God.

	Advaita (Monism)	Vishishtadvaita (Qualified Monism)	Dvaita (Dualism)
Propounded by →	Shankara	Ramanujacharya	Madhavacharya
Essence →	• There is only God • There is no difference between man and God • Everything is a manifestation of the same God and Godliness	• Man is a part or an aspect of God	• Man and God are entirely different and two distinct entities

"To me, it appears that purely from a logical standpoint, Advaita scores over the other two concepts. If we say God is omnipresent, all-pervasive, and infinite, where is the scope for anything else to exist?" Priya's reasoning was indeed sound.

"Brilliant! Difficult to fault that logic," agreed Varsha.

"Another way of interpreting the Advaita theory could be that there is just you and no one else. Even if faced with adversity and injustice in life, it's still you who will have to pick up the pieces and get going again. No point in hoping for divine intervention coming from some external source."

"For example, in cricket, a batsman may get hit on his body by a fast bowler, but he still has to gather himself to face the next ball. The certainty that he alone has to face the next ball and has to give it his all will make him simultaneously unafraid to face the next ball and also be free of worry for the consequences. Would that be a reasonable interpretation?" asked Virat.

> *"It is not the certainty that we are alone in facing life which gives us the courage. It is the realisation that we are no different from God that does so,"* said Rajan.

> *"What I like most about the Advaita theory is that it suggests each one of us has infinite possibilities within us. By stating that we are one and the same as God, it fills us with confidence and positive thinking. It teaches*

us to shed insecurity, think and dream big, identifying ourselves with the whole universe," said Rajan.

"Having said that, these concepts require much deeper study. My knowledge is too basic for me to comment beyond this."

Priya, Varsha and Virat bore a contemplative look on their faces as they listened to Rajan. Clearly, Advaita was great food for thought.

Section E

Sanatana Dharma and the Modern World

The sheer depth and sophistication of the ancient Indian thought, as reflected in several sacred Hindu texts, is truly magnificent and demonstrates an intellectual maturity that was way ahead of its era. These texts present a holistic view, covering not only spirituality but also ethics, social harmony, and a deep connection to the universe. Their messages encourage introspection, compassion, and a quest for knowledge, urging individuals to explore the nature of existence and their place within it, making Sanatana Dharma extremely relevant in the modern world.

This section covers the distinctive aspects that set Sanatana Dharma apart and why it is more than a conventional religion. It explains why all Indians can and should rightfully take immense pride in this priceless treasure.

Chapters in this Section:

23. The Sanatana List of Good and Bad Qualities

24. Why is Sanatana Dharma Truly Unique?

25. Sanatana and Liberalism – Two Sides of the Same Coin?

Chapter 23

The Sanatana List of Good and Bad Qualities

*First and foremost, you need to be a good citizen
of the world!*

One might wonder what explains the extraordinarily high tolerance shown by Hindus throughout their history towards other faiths, including faiths practised by the invaders of their land. Were Hindus a cowardly lot, who could not put up any resistance when they were sought to be converted to other faiths forcefully? Absolutely not. It is only through the sheer commitment and determination of successive generations of Hindus to preserve their religion and traditions that today Hinduism is the predominant religion in India, despite a thousand years of rule by invaders who practised and propagated other faiths.

It is also equally true that there were hardly any violent attacks by Hindus on the followers of other faiths and religions because of the latter's religion. This was primarily because of two reasons. One, the Sanatana Dharma texts never claim that the path suggested by them is the only path. Quite on the contrary, they say very explicitly that there are many paths to the 'Truth'. Second, the most important Sanatana scriptures specify **Non-violence** to be an extremely important attribute for the evolution of a human being. While the Yamas and Niyamas in the Vedas call for humans to practise non-violence in thoughts, words, and action, the Bhagavad Gita lists compassion (dayā), gentleness (mardavam), patience (kshamā), and non-hatred (adroha) as important qualities to be cultivated and nurtured by all human beings. These teachings of Sanatana Dharma have ingrained and entrenched certain values in Hindus over thousands of years, which in turn have made them extremely tolerant of differing views on matters of religion and spirituality.

Take a look at these Bhagavad Gita verses (one, two and three from Chapter XVI) that speak of twenty-six good (daivi) qualities or virtues one should imbibe and nurture within oneself:

अभयं सत्त्वसंशुद्धिर्ज्ञानयोगव्यवस्थिति:।
दानं दमश्च यज्ञश्च स्वाध्यायस्तप आर्जवम्॥ 1॥

अहिंसा सत्यमक्रोधस्त्याग: शान्तिरपैशुनम्|
दया भूतेष्वलोलुत्वं मार्दवं ह्रीरचापलम्|| 2||

तेज: क्षमा धृति: शौचमद्रोहोनातिमानिता|
भवन्ति सम्पदं दैवीमभिजातस्य भारत|| 3||

abhayaṁ sattva-sanśhuddhir jñāna-yoga-vyavasthitiḥ
dānaṁ damaśh cha yajñaśh cha svādhyāyas tapa
ārjavam

ahinsā satyam akrodhas tyāgaḥ śhāntir apaiśhunam
dayā bhūteṣhv aloluptvaṁ mārdavaṁ hrīr achāpalam

tejaḥ kṣhamā dhṛitiḥ śhaucham adroho nāti-mānitā
bhavanti sampadaṁ daivīm abhijātasya bhārata

The twenty-six attributes of a divine (*Daivi*) human being:

1. Fearlessness (*Abhayam*);

2. Purity of heart (*Sattva Samshuddhi*), which essentially means good intentions;

3. Steadfastness in devotion to knowledge (*Jnana Yoga*);

4. Charity (*Daana*), which also involves restraining one's instincts of acquisition and aggrandisement;

5. Restraint over one's senses (*Dama*), so as not to become their slave;

6. Regular prayers, sadhana or meditation (*Yajna*);

7. Study of the scriptures (*Swadhyaya*);

8. Austerity (*Tapas*), developing the power to withstand hardships like thirst, hunger, cold and heat;

9. Uprightness (*Aarjavam*), or being honest and straight-forward;

10. Non-violence (*Ahimsa*) or not harming anything or anybody;

11. Truthfulness (*Satyam*);

12. Even temper (*Akrodha*) or control over anger;

13. Sacrifice (*Tyaaga*) or a willingness to give up something for greater good;

14. Quietude (Shanti) which means maintaining peace within;

15. Soft and pleasant speech (*Apaishunam*) or unmalicious tongue;

16. Compassion (*Dayaa*), which includes compassion towards all beings and nature;

17. Non-covetousness (*Aloluptvam*), or not being greedy;

18. Gentleness (*Mardavam*);

19. Modesty or Humility (*Hrih*);

20. Steadiness or not being fickle minded (*Achaapalam*);

21. Vigour (*Tejas*) or glowing with sharpness, brightness and high energy;

22. Forgiving (*Kshamaa*);

23. Fortitude (*Dhriti*);

24. Cleanliness (*Shoucham*) or hygiene;

25. Absence of malice, treachery, ill feeling (*Adroha*);

26. Absence of excess pride (*Na-ati-manita*);

The very next verse (Verse four from Chapter XVI of the Bhagavad Gita) also speaks of the five bad (demonic) qualities that one needs to shed or stay away from:

दम्भो दर्पोऽभिमानश्च क्रोध: पारुष्यमेव च|
अज्ञानं चाभिजातस्य पार्थ सम्पदमासुरीम्||

dambho darpo 'bhimānaśh cha krodhaḥ pāruṣhyam eva cha
ajñānaṁ chābhijātasya pārtha sampadam āsurīm

The five demonic qualities that a human being should avoid:

1. Hypocrisy (*Dambha*) - portraying oneself to be smarter, wiser and more accomplished than one really is, or trying to cover for one's misdeeds by portraying oneself as noble and God fearing;

2. Arrogance (*Darpa*) leading to conceit (*Abhimanah*) - excess pride over one's possessions, and the subsequent putting down of others who may not have what one has;

3. Anger (*Krodha*);

4. Insolence (*Parushya*) or harshness, either at the body or at a speech level;

5. Delusion (*Ajnanam*) which means not knowing which action is right, and which action is to be avoided;

The most remarkable thing about these thirty-one qualities (twenty six good and five bad) is that barring one, the remaining thirty have absolutely nothing to do with religion or God. They all pertain to character building for human beings, which would most certainly lead to a better world. This is yet another instance wherein one can see clearly that Sanatana Dharma is not merely a religion, but a way of life.

The above is also a reflection of the type of values Sanatana Dharma has tried to inculcate and promote, and its emphasis on making society more peaceful, harmonious and progressive.

"Man, that is quite a list. I don't think it is possible for anyone to have all those qualities!" *exclaimed Varsha.*

"That is the complete list of good qualities a perfect human being should have, and the bad qualities such a human should be free of. That is what our scriptures expect each one of us to strive for and progress towards," responded Rajan, with a smile.

"If our society indeed believed in imbibing such good qualities, how come India is where it is today, with respect to poverty, illiteracy, human development and so on?" *asked Varsha.*

"In my personal opinion, it is precisely because we did not take care to include and highlight the best of our ancient wisdom in our school curriculum. Our school and university education is still not very different from what the British left us with. And politics too has played a role in keeping it that way for almost eight decades that have passed since our independence," opined Rajan.

"I agree with almost all points, except the one about regular prayers," *said Virat, almost predictably.*

"That is the only one, out of the thirty-odd points above, that is somewhat linked to God or worship. Even that can be interpreted as sadhana or meditation."

"The overwhelming focus seems to be on promoting the values of non-violence, compassion, peace, harmony, truthfulness and personal evolution, and on curbing all those aspects of our behaviour that could lead to conflict. No wonder the Hindus have shown such high tolerance throughout their history towards other faiths and even towards atheism. It is also no surprise that several new faiths like Sikhism, Buddhism and Jainism were not only born, but could survive and even thrive, in a land full of Hindus. This would have been unimaginable in those times elsewhere, and even today quite unimaginable in many parts of the world." Rajan's pride in his Hindu identity was unmistakable.

Chapter 24

Why Is Sanatana Dharma Truly Unique?

You have inherited some truly precious thoughts. Value them, preserve them, and spread them as your contribution towards a better world!

- Sanatana Dharma is closer to the word 'Spirituality' and is wider in scope than the word 'Religion'. It encourages seeking rather than believing. Many of its scriptures are in question-answer form. At times, it even seems to question the very existence of God.

- Sanatana Dharma

  - has not been founded by any one person;

  - does not believe in any single form of God;

  - is not governed by a single scripture or religious book;

- is not governed by any human authority, like a religious head or organised body.

- Sanatana Dharma does not prescribe any ONE way of worship or rituals, calling it the only way. It defines the purpose of life as attaining a state of ultimate and permanent happiness and suggests several means to achieve it.

- Sanatana Dharma allows one to interpret God in more ways than one: from the concept of a Personal God to God as a formless infinite expanse of the universe. It lets one imagine and relate to God as a caring parent, an affectionate friend, a guru, and so on.

- Sanatana Dharma accepts even atheists and agnostics and gives them the freedom to explore spirituality with an open mind.

- While there are many aspects that make Sanatana Dharma distinctly different, four of them stand out. Together, these four aspects make Sanatana Dharma truly unique. Every student of Hinduism and India should know and always remember these four fundamentally unique aspects of Sanatana Dharma:

    1. No Hindu scripture claims to be the only truth. Nor does any Hindu scripture say that the Hindu alone will attain God. In fact, Hinduism clearly recognises the fact that while the truth (God) is one, there could be several ways to reach that

truth. One of the key quotes from the Sanatana scriptures says, '***Ekam Sat Vipra Bahudha Vadanti***'. This quote from the Upanishads means: "***That which exists is ONE; sages call it by various names.***" This idea is ingrained in the civilisation of India for thousands of years, which in turn is reflected in the unqualified acceptance shown by the Hindus towards other religions that emerged much later.

2. Nowhere **does Sanatana Dharma advocate mistreatment of, or discrimination or violence against atheists or non believers.** Sanatana Dharma co-existed with Charvaka, an Indian school of philosophy which rejected the Vedas and the concepts of rebirth, Karma, liberation (Moksha) and the immortality of the Self. The Charvaka philosophy predates 150 BCE. It rejected the very concept of God and spoke of the world of religion and spirituality as an aberration. The Brihaspati Sutra is the most important book of this school of thought, according to which the material world was the only reality. The mere existence of such a philosophy almost two thousand years back is an important symbol of Hindu tolerance. In most other parts of the world those days, preachers of such a philosophy would have been punished severely.

There are many shlokas in the Sanatana scriptures which pray for the whole universe, without distinguishing between believers and non-believers. A few examples: Atmano Mokshartham Jagat Hitaya Cha (for the salvation of our individual self and for the well-being of all on earth), *Sarve Bhavantu Sukhinah* (may all be happy), *Loka Samasta Sukhino Bhavantu* (may everyone in the whole world be happy), and many more.

3. Sanatana Dharma does not recognize the concept of Conversions. Nowhere does it advocate converting people from other belief systems into its fold, nor is there a defined process for conversions in its scriptures. In fact, the Sanatana scriptures do not even advocate propagating Sanatana Dharma. Verses 67 and 68 from Chapter XVIII of the Bhagavad Gita specifically advise against sharing the wisdom with those who have no interest in, or are predisposed towards disrespecting, the same.

4. The Sanatana scriptures very specifically list **'Non-Violence (Ahimsa)'** as key to achieving the purpose of life, and **'Non-Hatred (Adroha)'** as a key quality of a good human being. The Mahabharata verse 'Ahimsa Paramo Dharma' describes non-violence as an important duty of man. That is why Mahatma Gandhi said, "I

believe that the essence of Hinduism is truth and non-violence." He also said, "Non-violence is common to all religions, but it has found the highest expression and application in Hinduism." The only situation where the use of force could be justified in *Sanatana Dharma* is during a *Dharma Yudh*, when the core Sanatana values of tolerance, justice, non-violence, compassion, service, love etc. are themselves under threat.

The above points clearly set Sanatana Dharma apart.

"Would not every religion have something unique to offer? What is the purpose of highlighting the unique aspects of Sanatana Dharma? Are we trying to claim some superiority? If so, don't you think that itself would promote differences between communities?" *Virat's tone was both blunt and sharp.*

"I think there are some things you need to know as general knowledge. Just as you try to gain some basic knowledge about your country, you should also know the basic message of your religion, irrespective of whether you are a believer or a non believer. Otherwise, you run the risk of being made to feel defensive needlessly about certain aspects of your identity."

"There are certain uniquely praiseworthy and special aspects of Sanatana Dharma, which we should all know about. Sensible Hindus will use it to develop confidence in their identity, without letting it make them arrogant or feel superior."

"As for following the teachings of Sanatana Dharma, it is completely a different matter. That should be, and will be, only your decision. This approach is also in the true spirit of Sanatana Dharma. As a caring parent, I just want your decision to be well-informed and well-considered."

"You have listed many unique aspects of Sanatana Dharma through all your notes. Which ones do you feel are truly praiseworthy?" Varsha seemed keen to discuss the subject further.

"The last point in my notes speaks of four fundamentally unique aspects of Sanatana Dharma, viz.,

1	**Acceptance of the legitimacy of all other religions**
2	**Acceptance of the right of atheists and non-believers to coexist**
3	**Shunning proactive and institutional attempts to convert people from other faiths, especially those using force and allurements**
4	**Adopting non-violence as a core tenet**

If the whole world adopts these four principles, it would put a permanent end to all religious conflicts in this world."

"More than 3000 years ago or possibly even much earlier, when savages still roamed parts of the world, our ancestors decided to inculcate such deeply tolerant values in society which have survived through several millennia. This is truly amazing and remarkable. This is the sole reason why we Hindus have such a high degree of tolerance even today and have no issues living peacefully with followers of other faiths."

"And it is not just tolerance and acceptance. It is almost as if Hindus are 'genetically' programmed to respect all Gods, including those of other religions. It is normal to see Hindus bowing their heads and paying their obeisance even as they are walking past a dargah, a church, a gurdwara or a Buddhist monastery."

"If non violence is a core value practised by all Hindus, why did the war of Mahabharata take place?" *Virat was unwilling to take Rajan's points at face value.*

"I think the teachings of any religion have to be seen as distinct from the actions of its individual followers, or for that matter, a group of followers. There would be good and bad people in any community. In Mahabharata, the Kauravas led by Duryodhana, were acting completely against the teachings of Sanatana

Dharma. If the Kauravas were let off unchallenged, it would have resulted in the death of Dharma itself, and its values of tolerance, justice, non-violence, compassion and service. So the war against the Kauravas and their evil designs became a Dharma Yudh. Only a Dharma Yudh justifies the use of force as per Sanatana Dharma."

"Let us say you have created a free society where everyone has the freedom to decide for himself on matters of faith, beliefs and practises. Now let us say a group that looks down upon and insults atheists or agnostics is gaining ground in your society. Does it not then become necessary for you to stand up and fight this group if you are committed to preserving the freedom that you desire for everyone in your society?"

"But then what about the ultra conservative groups that take the law into their hands in the name of stopping or curtailing certain social behaviours, which they unilaterally term to be irreligious and indecent?" *Priya was worried about some hooliganism that she had seen on the TV news the previous week.*

"Such behaviour has no sanction in Sanatana Dharma and is clearly against its teachings. These are matters of law and order that need to be addressed by the government. If a government fails to do so, you have the right to do everything possible to vote them out in the next election."

Chapter 25

Sanatana Dharma and Liberalism – Two Sides of the same Coin?

The survival and growth of Hindu philosophy could be key to a truly liberal and tolerant world!

The world of religion needs a greater dose of freedom. Most of the religious world is dominated by authorities who demand compliance with rules. Fear has become the chief emotion that drives people towards religion. People seek solace in religion when confronted with fear of personal failures and setbacks and comply with religious practises and rituals out of fear of authorities like priests and self-appointed custodians of different religions. Many people are even afraid of a backlash from the Almighty should they fail to comply. In an environment that is enveloped so overwhelmingly by fear, where is the room left for any seeking and exploration?

Spiritual seekers can seek and explore alone, all by themselves in solitude. But without a supporting ecosystem, that journey would be infinitely tougher and take much longer, with seekers having to reinvent the wheel again and again. An active and free spiritual ecosystem would make that journey easier, more joyful, and much more effective.

What is an 'active and free' spiritual ecosystem? It is an ecosystem wherein a beginner can instantly dip into and draw from thousands of years of work. It would have scores of experts to talk to, debate with and learn from. It would have an extensive body of scriptural work to study and accept or reject. It would have many places of supposedly high spiritual energies, wherein a seeker can meditate and search for peace and enlightenment.

Let us take a look at the Sanatana Dharma ecosystem, against the backdrop of the above.

- The Sanatana Dharma ecosystem is both extensive and rich in diversity. There is no single religious authority that controls Sanatana Dharma. There are hundreds of schools of philosophy, thousands of gurus, and lakhs of saints.

- The scriptures are vast and provide a range of fascinating interpretations, sometimes contradicting one another. And you are free to give your own interpretations too, and even propagate the same!

- There are thousands of places of worship, offering a wide variety of experiences ranging from grand ceremonies, loud chanting and singing, to silent and deep meditation in solitude.

- The rituals and religious practises change from place to place and often from house to house.

- There is no compulsion on anybody to believe in or follow anything. There is no discrimination against non-believers.

- You could go in and out of any school of thought or the teachings of any guru or any particular set of rituals and practises without having to explain anything to anybody.

- Consider this verse in Bhagavad Gita:

Chapter XVIII, Verse 63:

इति ते ज्ञानमाख्यातं गुह्याद्गुह्यतरं मया।
विमृश्यैतदशेषेण यथेच्छसि तथा कुरु॥

Iti te jñānam ākhyātaṁ guhyād guhyataraṁ mayā
vimṛiśhyaitad aśheṣheṇa yathechchhasi tathā kuru

Translation

"Thus, I have imparted to you this knowledge, which is more precious than any secret. Reflect upon it deeply, and then act according to your will."

This verse comes towards the conclusion of the Bhagavad Gita. After revealing to Arjuna the most precious wisdom about life's purpose and how to attain it, the Lord does not insist or even expect that his pupil Arjuna, a mere human, should comply with his teachings without applying his independent thought on the same. He specifically tells Arjuna that what He has revealed to him is the most precious, rarest of rare wisdom. And then goes on to add that Arjuna should now reflect on this deeply and decide whether to accept it or not. Just pause and think about how our ancient sages have visualised the relationship between God and man. This is such a great example of how Sanatana Dharma not just accepts or even encourages, but in fact insists upon, free and independent thinking amongst its followers. In this Bhagavad Gita verse, this is insisted upon by none other than God himself!

In Sanatana Dharma, nothing is beyond question. There is no concept of blasphemy or sacrilege and no established convention of punishments for the same. There could be individual and stray reactions, but no institutional backlash. Most Hindus just ignore such acts.

And then you have the 129th hymn from the 10th mandala of Rigveda. The hymn is a deep contemplation into how this whole creation could have started. What was the original cause, the primal trigger, the causeless cause? What existed before that? So on and so forth. And finally, after this deep and intense contemplation, the hymn wonders who could possibly know about these things. And then, in a dramatic and almost sacrilegious twist, it ends like this:

> "...Who truly knows? And who can really say? Whence did it all originate? And how did creation unfold? The Gods themselves came later than creation, so who knows the source of this great creation? Who knows whence this creation originated? He, whether He shaped it or whether He did not, He, who observes it all from the highest heavens knows - **or perhaps even He does not know.**"

Such is the uninhibited, free and fearless enquiry that Sanatana Dharma, not merely allows, but encourages and even expects from spiritual seekers. A free-spirited seeker and explorer can dip into this vast spiritual ecosystem, consume whatever he wants, accept whatever appeals to him, reject whatever does not, and continue to express freely and engage intensely with thousands of others who are extremely knowledgeable in different schools of thought within the Sanatana umbrella. Any genuine spiritual seeker, who is not yet ready to submit entirely to a particular belief system, would find the very prospect of such engagement extremely motivating.

People who seek a more liberal world need to ponder this a bit more deeply, even if they themselves are atheists with no interest in matters of religion and spirituality. And just like they speak about the need for press freedom and freedom of expression, they should also speak about the need for freedom in matters of religion and spirituality. After all, the number of people who find the need for religious and spiritual solace is likely to be much bigger than the many micro-interest groups, whose cause the liberals regularly and very rightly espouse. Promoting liberalism within the universally practised activity of religion could yield substantially bigger and better results in the pursuit of a more liberal world. That alone should be reason enough for many to revisit their stance on Sanatana Dharma.

"Never thought of the liberties of religious believers and spiritual seekers. Always saw liberals as atheists. I now wonder why. After all, being liberal is a completely

different aspect from a person's religious or spiritual orientation," wondered Varsha.

"You are not alone in this confusion. Many people assume that all religious persons would be conservative or illiberal in their thinking.

"We need to speak up for the liberties of the millions of seekers and believers in our society. And we need to resist any change in our society that slowly ebbs away at these liberties over time. And these threats could come from both within and outside the fold of Sanatana Dharma." Rajan's views were good food for thought.

"I remember once Kishan came to college after visiting a temple, with a small tika on his forehead. He was not conscious about it. However, everyone around became quite uncomfortable and made him doubly uncomfortable. When Kishan realised the 'problem', he went to the washroom and returned after washing his forehead clean. Looking back, I now feel that the reaction by my group of friends was certainly not a liberal reaction. Coming to think of it, a tattoo was ok, but not a tika! There is considerable food for thought there for all those involved in that incident." *Virat's relating the point to a real-life incident made it even more clear to all.*

Section F
Summary, Takeaways and Conclusion

This section outlines a mindset that could help us keep depression and negative thinking away throughout our lives. It also presents a quick summary of Sanatana philosophy that could help us effectively articulate its core essence to anyone interested within a few minutes.

This is followed by suggested takeaways that the readers could consider incorporating into their lives. The closing conversations among the characters also bring the 'family story' to a satisfying close.

Chapters in this Section

26. Atmano Mokshartham Jagat Hitaya Cha
(आत्मनो मोक्षार्थम् जगत् हिताय च)

27. The Ten-Minute Summary

28. Takeaways for the Rajan Family

29. A Festive Feeling

Chapter 26

Atmano Mokshartham Jagat Hitaya Cha
(आत्मनो मोक्षार्थम् जगत् हिताय च)

A set of simple yet profound twin-goals that could keep your life lit up brightly until the very end!

Driven by our needs, duties, and desires, we are constantly chasing many goals at every stage of our lives. It is only to be expected in such a relentless chase of multiple goals that we might fail to achieve some of them. After all, while our efforts towards a particular goal may lie in our hands, the outcomes are not in our control.

Some of these individual failures could devastate us and push us into a state of low self-esteem and depression. To avoid this possibility or to mitigate the adverse effects of failures and setbacks in our lives, **an**

'overarching' goal or goals that inspire us throughout our lifetime can be of great help.

In other words, while chasing multiple short and medium-term goals, if we are always committed at a deeper level to some enduring and meaningful goals, we will never ever feel totally defeated and worthless. These wider goals should be such that they provide us with a genuine chance to celebrate small victories every day. These should help us remain positive always, irrespective of all the other challenges we face in life.

It is in this context that the Rig Veda verse 'Atmano Mokshartham - Jagat Hitaya Cha' (आत्मनो मोक्षार्थम् जगत् हिताय च) assumes significance. It suggests a twofold purpose for human life: (1) to try to attain ultimate happiness or Ananda through perfection in individual life, and (2) to work for the welfare of the world. This was supposedly stated by Swami Ramakrishna Paramahamsa to Swami Vivekananda and is the vision and mission statement of the Ramakrishna Order, the monastic lineage that carries on its work through the Ramakrishna Math and the Ramakrishna Mission.

No matter what our state is, there will always be something we can do for both 'Atmano Mokshartham' (self-improvement/evolution) and 'Jagat Hitaya Cha' (welfare of others). Even a bedridden person can (a) acquire knowledge or work on his mind for 'Atmano Mokshartham' and (b) make someone happy by merely being a good and compassionate listener, for 'Jagat Hitaya Cha'. Therefore, one can never ever fail completely or feel totally worthless with respect to either 'Atmano Mokshartham' or 'Jagat Hitaya Cha'. That is why they are great lifelong goals for us to adopt. They can motivate and inspire us throughout our lives, constantly enhancing our feeling of self-worth, even in the most challenging of times.

The two goals are also mutually complementary. If you are keen to contribute towards the welfare of others, you need to first empower yourself and also keep yourself in a positive frame of mind, both of which are integral to *Atmano Mokshartham*. In other words, personal development through *Atmano Mokshartham* is crucial to be able to make a meaningful impact in "Jagat Hitaya Cha". Similarly, any act towards *Jagat Hitaya Cha* enhances your feeling of self-worth and inner peace, resulting in *Atmano Mokshartham*!

Let us now see how widely we can interpret these two phrases *Atmano Mokshartham* and *Jagat Hitaya Cha*.

Atmano Mokshartham

Our scriptures say that to achieve the life purpose of Ananda, a good and healthy body and a calm and peaceful mind are key. Therefore, almost anything we do to make ourselves happy, healthy, and empowered might be capable of being directly or indirectly connected with 'Atmano Mokshartham'.

- Getting a healthy body would include good food, exercise, and sleep.

- Calming the mind could include any pursuit that can make us happy and relax our mind, including sensory pleasures pursued in moderation, as referred to in the Gita.

- Empowering ourselves through education and learning, earning money, pursuing material goals could all be covered under 'Atmano Mokshartham', so long as we are clear that we will eventually put our material possessions to good use, like

  - Making ourselves and our near and dear ones happy

  - Spreading happiness and empowerment among others

Jagat Hitaya Cha

Strictly speaking, the welfare of the world is the 'welfare of others'. Since nobody can do welfare to the whole world, making even one other person happy could be seen as 'Jagat Hitaya Cha'. Depending on our current station in life, our state of empowerment, the breadth of our vision, and the largeness of our heart, that 'other person' could be any of the following:

- Our immediate family (parents, spouse, children);

- Siblings

- Friends and relatives

- Our colleagues

- People who help us in our daily life, like our maid or our office staff;

- The economically challenged, the physically challenged, victims of any accident, disaster, mishap, or conflict;

- Our social communities, the residents of our locality;

- Our countrymen

- The whole of humankind, or even the entire living world.

The geography of our influence (through our welfare, help or support) could be just our home, our locality, our city, our country, or the whole world!

So our interpretation of what constitutes 'Atmano Mokshartham and Jagat Hitaya Cha' could be based on our current state, preferences, and priorities. And as we evolve and get more and more empowered, our interpretation could also evolve and widen suitably. That is why 'Atmano Mokshartham Jagat Hitaya Cha' is a fantastic set of goals to adopt. We will never ever feel helpless that we can do nothing towards these goals, and therefore it can keep us always feeling potent, impactful, and motivated.

"Are you saying we could even classify eating in a restaurant under 'Atmano Mokshartham'? Don't you think that is too much of a stretch?" *Varsha sounded amused by this possibility.*

"If you word it that way, it does sound like a stretch," admitted Rajan.

"However, our scriptures have recognised the importance of both Artha and Kama in our lives and do not bar us from pursuing pleasures or wealth. The only rider is moderation. Please remember the Bhagavad Gita verses that we discussed in our note on detachment."

"Man needs to empower himself and be in a good mental state to be able to contribute constructively towards society. How can an utterly unhappy or frustrated man help others? Or for that matter, how can such a man meditate or attempt spiritual evolution?"

"That is why I believe that pursuing pleasures that keep you in a happy and positive state of mind should be fine, so long as you exercise moderation and avoid becoming a slave to such pleasures."

"And taking care of your children is 'Jagat Hitaya Cha'? That is such a narrow interpretation of doing welfare for others!" *said Priya in disapproval.*

"Taking care of one's children includes the responsibility of correct upbringing to ensure that one raises good citizens, who will be assets, and not a burden, to society. In that sense, taking care of one's children is indeed Jagat Hitaya Cha."

"Further, an entirely Tamasic man's innate nature would make him shun even his basic duties, like providing for or protecting his immediate family. I have known people like that. Our scriptures say that every man should assess his basic nature and strive to move to the next level. A completely Tamasic man should try to become as Rajasic as possible. Trying to make him Sattvic would be futile and counterproductive."

"But then don't you think such a narrow and restricted definition of 'Jagat Hitaya Cha' would discourage the rich from giving back to society at scale?" *asked Varsha.*

"Whatever I have said in this context so far is more to make you see why 'Atmano Mokshartham Jagat Hitaya Cha' can be adopted as lifelong goals by anybody, no matter how poor or disempowered. Irrespective of your current station or position in life, there is always something you can do towards both 'Atmano

Mokshartham' and 'Jagat Hitaya Cha'. You will never feel totally helpless in the pursuit of these two goals if you adopt them in the true spirit. Anyone who does so will always feel that he is very much in the game with a definite chance to 'achieve' every day," explained Rajan.

"On your point about the need for the rich to open their purse strings to the poor, there is no doubt that as a community the Indian upper middle class and rich can do much more. I would like to see more Indians committing to give something back to society. The affluent in India, with a handful of exceptions, hardly give anything back. People try to accumulate even in their old age, only to leave behind a large amount of wealth for their already rich children. This mindset needs to change.' Rajan's observations stemmed from his genuine concern for the underprivileged and the high levels of inequality in society.

"All able-bodied and even reasonably well-to-do adults should make giving back to society an integral part of their lives, especially in a country like India, where even today millions are severely deprived," Priya's views sounded more like a passionate appeal, which found resonance with the other three.

Chapter 27

The Ten-Minute Summary

When your French colleague from your company's San Jose office asked you, "What is the core message of Hinduism?" how did you fare? Well, you don't have to struggle anymore.

If someone asks us to summarise the core message of Sanatana Dharma in ten minutes, how can we do it? Here is a quick summary:

- Life's purpose is to reach a state of ultimate and permanent happiness, or Ananda. Ananda is a state of mind that lies within us, and not in any external beings or objects.

- We are more than our body and mind. At our core, we are the Atman, which is a speck of God inside us. This Atman is our real self.

- All our sense organs are outward-facing. Therefore, we desire and chase external beings and objects on the false notion that these can make us happy. In reality, while they may give us momentary joy, obsessing over such external beings and objects can give us only pain and suffering in the long run. We are unable to realise this because of our ignorance, or Maya.

- It is Maya that makes us overlook the fundamental truth that everything in this world is transient. All our worldly possessions, including our near and dear ones, are not 'ours'. We own nothing and no one. Our time with everything and everyone is limited. This applies also to one's opinions, fears, likes, dislikes and expectations. If we get very attached to these, we are bound to end up as frustrated and bitter people.

- It is Maya that keeps us trapped in a feeling of incompleteness, making us seek many things from this world like true friends, appreciation from others, respect in society, etc. This, in turn, keeps us submerged in a life of deep attachments, fears, insecurities, greed, frustrations, jealousy, ego and anger.

- However, when we identify our true self, we understand that completeness is right within us in the form of our Atman, our true essence. God exists within us as our Atman, and that we in fact are God.

- The way to overcome Maya is to work on our minds using one or more of the four paths of Yoga. These are the paths of selfless action (Karma Yoga), unconditional love (Bhakti Yoga), ultimate knowledge (Jnana Yoga), or high willpower (Raja Yoga). All of them involve sustained efforts.

- These paths help us overcome negative qualities like obsessive desire for material objects, greed, possessiveness, anger, arrogance, ego, jealousy and depression, by cultivating and nurturing positive qualities like love, compassion, selflessness, non-violence, honesty, humility and the right amount of detachment.

- Eventually all paths take us deep within ourselves, through mindfulness and deep meditation, to experience the Atman or God within us.

- Once we overcome Maya completely, we stop seeing ourselves and the world as different. We stop seeing differences and see the whole universe as one extended existence. We feel one with the whole universe, with God. We feel complete within ourselves and reach the state of Ananda.

- Our attainment of Ananda is inevitable and may happen within one lifetime or many, depending on our Karma, which comprises all our thoughts, words and actions. Every Karma of ours creates a reaction that manifests itself as an experience, either good or bad depending on the original Karma. These manifestations have to be experienced and exhausted fully through one or more births for us to reach the state of Ananda.

- Death does not mark our end. Death merely means that we have undergone and exhausted the experiences earmarked for our present life. However, our Atman continues its journey towards God or Ananda through a new birth in a new body.

- Upon reaching Ananda, there are no further rebirths.

- Ananda is a state of merger with God, a permanent state of ultimate happiness and peace.

"In my 30s, I was working for a multinational company, headquartered in Germany. During one of my trips to Germany, a German colleague asked me to explain the core essence of Sanatana Dharma philosophy. To my own dismay, I struggled. Not because I did not know, but because I could not put the different elements into a concise and coherent narrative. I am sure he must have felt that I did not know enough about my own religion."

"I realised subsequently that I was not alone in this inadequacy. If you ask a random set of Hindus to explain the essence of Hindu philosophy within five or ten minutes, I suspect you might see them struggle. It is not because they do not know. In fact, many of them might be living their lives as per Sanatana Dharma. However, almost all of them would struggle to give you a well-rounded 360° summary as a quick takeaway."

"This could be because our scriptures do not advocate the active propagation of Sanatana Dharma. However, having spent over 30 years working as a corporate executive, I simply had to prepare an 'Executive Summary'," said Rajan with a smile.

After pausing for a few seconds, he said, "Well, that was the last of my notes," to be greeted by a spontaneous round of loud applause from Priya, Varsha and Virat.

"Your notes were so useful, Rajan. Looking back, I can see the logic in the way the notes were sequenced. The topics *flowed smoothly from one to the other, and at the end, there is a feeling of some sort of natural conclusion. I do not think I could have got this sort of a 360° overview of Sanatana Dharma and its messages so easily, without your notes and these discussions." Priya's admiration was both genuine and reflective of her pride in her husband.*

"I agree," said Virat, adding, "I have made my own notes of all our discussions. I suggest you three list your takeaways too and share them with me. I am keen to prepare a summary of key takeaways that could apply to all of us. Let us do one last round of discussions next Sunday, which is Appa's birthday, on our joint takeaways from these discussions."

"Yes," the loud and unanimous response from the other three revealed their delight in hearing Virat's comments.

It was already 10 pm. Varsha retired to her room. There was some office work that she had to complete quickly. A Google meeting was scheduled to start in 30 minutes, and as usual, Varsha wanted to jot down the key points on a whiteboard stuck to the wall above her worktable. However, she noticed that her marker pen was missing. "Virat must have taken it to his room," she thought.

She went into Virat's room and found her marker pen on his table. As she picked it up, her eyes fell on the beautiful idol of Lord Vishnu that her mother had bought for Virat, prominently displayed on the table. It had gone missing for a few years. Its reappearance on Virat's table brought a smile to Varsha's face.

Chapter 28

Takeaways for the Rajan Family

This was not just another Sunday. It was Rajan's birthday.
Both Rajan and Priya had spent more time in their puja
room today and were surprised to see Varsha join them too
for a good fifteen minutes. There was a feeling of greater peace
in the house. Priya had prepared an elaborate meal. Varsha
and Rajan had lent her a helping hand. Virat chose to join
them just in time for lunch, busy as he was in finalising the
takeaways from their several weeks of discussion. Virat was
keen to present the 'Takeaways Note' on Rajan's birthday,
for he was sure it would make his father immensely happy.

The lunch was delightfully sumptuous. Post lunch,
the family settled down with their dessert bowls for the

discussions on Virat's notes on takeaways, which read as follows:

- The purpose of our lives is to attain and retain a state of maximum happiness.

- This **ultimate happiness is already within us, waiting to be experienced.** It is not in anything outside.

- **The key to experiencing this ultimate happiness is to work on the mind and master the art of being calm, yet alert, at all times.** This is a skill that can be perfected through practice.

- Determine your goals through a two-step process

  - **Step One** - Adopt "Self-Empowerment / Evolution" (Atmano Mokshartham) and "Welfare of Others" (Jagat Hitaya Cha) as your two principal overarching goals that would be a running theme throughout your life.

  - **Step Two** - Determine and align all your other goals under either of these two goals, directly or indirectly.

  - Working on your person (body and mind), career (money and position of influence), family (marriage, children, parents) and social equations (meaningful network) could all come within the ambit of "Self-Empowerment/Evolution".

- Likewise, loving and caring for your near and dear ones, your community, the poor and needy, your country etc. could all be categorised under "Welfare of Others".

- Work on your body and mind using Raja Yoga.

  - Body: Actively work towards achieving good health. Exercise regularly. Sync your diet and exercise routine with your personal health goals.

  - **Mind: Actively work to achieve a default state of mind that is 'calm, yet alert'. Practise the following regularly.**

    1. **Pranayama**

    2. **Meditation**

    3. **Witnessing Your Mind**

    These are perhaps the most important things that you can possibly do to attain and retain a state of maximum happiness.

- Use the three Jnana Yoga steps of Shravanam, Mananam, and Nidhidhyasanam[21] for effective learning in all your knowledge-gaining quests, whether they pertain to work, hobbies, or life.

- Try to adopt the teachings of Karma Yoga in all your work:

---

21 Three stages of learning as explained in Chapter 14 "Jnana Yoga - Path of Knowledge and Wisdom"

- Set challenging work goals to kindle within yourself the maximum motivation, inspiration, and energy regarding your work, so that the work becomes fun.

- Put in your best in planning and execution. After all, your 'free will-driven', determined effort is more important than your fate.

- Enjoy the chase of your work goals so that you can reap happiness and learnings from your work. If a goal gets difficult to achieve, use your creativity to do things differently, and also to do different things.

- **Use your work interactions as drills to improve the quality of your mind and its response to different stimuli, including stressful situations. Watch your mind during these interactions to reduce conflict and maintain calm.**

- Note and feel good about the everyday improvements that you make in your efforts and approach.

- Do not obsess excessively about the outcomes. Even if you miss a goal, do not miss the lessons.

- Enjoy and celebrate your growth both as a person and as a professional through the goal chase.

- Use the concept of a Personal God and Bhakti Yoga to nurture your emotions, and to cultivate and nurture love in your heart. The quality of your love and compassion will evolve, and this will reflect positively in all your personal relationships.

- Identify your predominant Guna mix and work on changing it for the better: from Tamasic to Rajasic, from Rajasic to Sattvic, and from Sattvic to a Gunatita. Remember that more often than not, it is your Gunas that drive your Karma. The Gita says 'even the wise are helpless when driven by their Gunas'. So constantly watch and understand your innate Gunas and keep improving them. Work hard to overcome ego, anger, jealousy, selfishness and greed. Do not give up.

- Enjoy the material and sensory pleasures that appeal to you (within generally accepted social norms), but make sure you do not become a slave to such pleasures. Exercise moderation to the extent that at all times, your intellect (and not an enslaved mind) is in control. Draw your own reasonable lines regarding what amounts to excess, and always stop short of such excess. Mind you, these lines may shift voluntarily, by themselves, as you (and your 'desires') evolve.

- Do your duties without fail and improve your self-worth. These would include your duties towards your immediate family, friends, relatives, local community, your nation, humankind and the world as a whole. Serve the needy and incorporate service and charity into your priorities.

- Follow the dos and don'ts as set out under *Yama* and *Niyama*[22].

- Imbibe and grow the twenty-six good qualities and shed the five bad qualities listed in the Gita, for your personal progress and evolution as a human being.[23]

- As a part of your commitment to the 'Welfare of Others', do your best to protect and preserve the freedom in spiritual exploration that Sanatana Dharma offers. Rise up to resist and fight whenever this freedom is threatened.

- In every challenging situation, remind yourself that it is your 'free will driven' effort, and your willpower, that will shape your success or failure more than your fate. If your past karma has been bad, you might need to work harder than others for your current happiness and success.

---

22 Dos and don'ts specified in Chapter 16 "Raja Yoga – Path of Willpower and Mind Control"

23 Refer to Chapter 23: The Sanatana list of good and bad qualities

- The above approach would not only help you achieve your short- and medium-term life goals but also continuously strengthen you from within. **This, in turn, would progressively take you towards a stable state of mind that is calm yet alert. That alone is the guarantee of your sustained happiness.**

"Wow! It is clear now, more than ever before, as to why Sanatana Dharma is a way of life, and not merely a religion!" Varsha's admiration for what her brother had penned was spontaneous.

"I must admit, while my faith was unshakeable, I had never applied my thoughts to the spiritual aspects of Sanatana Dharma. I derived my peace and happiness from my religious practises and was content with that. These discussions, and now this final note from Virat, have opened new vistas to explore and learn in the future. Feeling both excited and happy!" Priya's delight was sincere.

"I must confess I had a cynical view of Sanatana Dharma, which I now realise was born out of my ignorance about its core messages. I now feel that while one can praise anything spontaneously, one should not be critical of any school of thought without reasonable knowledge," added Virat.

"*That is the problem I see in many within our circles these days. They might find some Hindu practises or rituals illogical and would then extend that negative opinion to trash the entire philosophy, thereby permanently missing out on this priceless wisdom. It is like throwing the baby out with the bathwater,*" *said Priya.*

"*Irrespective of whether you choose to be a believer or not, how can you remain unaware of the basic philosophy of a religion with which over a billion people identify! I am glad that this unacceptable gap in my general knowledge has been bridged,*" *added Varsha.*

"*Most importantly, I no longer feel defensive about my identity as a Hindu. In fact, I am in awe of both the extent and quality of thought that our ancestors seem to have put into shaping our culture. I now feel nice and confident about being a Hindu and an Indian and want to let the detractors know about the same.*" *Virat's feelings reflected some regret that his ignorance had made him feel otherwise all these years.*

Rajan chose to remain silent. His gentle smile revealed his contentment.

Chapter 29

A Festive Feeling

"Appa, Neha and I are proposing to book the Vivekananda Hall for the wedding. It is a nice venue and has more than twenty rooms for important guests to stay the night before," said Virat.

"Why would anyone need to stay the previous night at the venue for a court wedding? It should be fine if we reach the venue a couple of hours before the reception. Shouldn't it?" asked Priya

"Amma, I have been thinking about our conversation regarding a court wedding versus a traditional wedding. On second thoughts, I am now keen to experience and enjoy the cultural aspects of our traditional wedding. I also feel I should not deny my near and dear ones the associated joy and fun. Neha's parents wish to come over this weekend to discuss the preparations with you and Appa," said Virat with a smile.

"Woo hoo! You promised to gift me an expensive dress for your wedding. Let us start the wedding shopping today itself," said a visibly excited Varsha.

"Sorry buddy. Neha wants me to accompany her to help her choose her wedding sarees. She also wants to check out some shops for my sherwani, which I shall wear during the evening reception. We are going to the North Star Mall today," said Virat as he left home, leaving the other members beaming in joy.

"Amma, I am going to my friend Swapna's house this evening and will stay overnight at her place. I will be back tomorrow morning after breakfast. Should be home by 10," said Varsha.

"Sunita aunty called. They have had a good harvest of mangoes on their farm this season. She is sending some over to us. Rohan will be coming in the evening to drop the mangoes," said Priya, concerned that Varsha wouldn't be around when Rohan arrived.

"Amma, incidentally, Swapna's parents will not be in town next weekend. On second thoughts, maybe it would be better for me to visit her then. It will be more fun," said Varsha, changing her mind instantly.

"That is a very good idea," said a smiling Rajan, winking mischievously at Priya.

Section G

Scriptures, References and Acknowledgements

This final section presents a brief overview of the key constituents of the Hindu Scriptures, highlighting those that this book has drawn from. It also lists the reference materials used for this book, besides acknowledging the significant contributions from various individuals to the making of this book.

Chapters in this Section:

30. The Hindu Scriptures

31. Acknowledgements & References

Chapter 30

The Hindu Scriptures

*The ocean of creations that make up the world
of 'Hindu Scriptures'!*

This section is recommended only for those who are inclined to get informed about the principal constituents of the Hindu scriptures. This will also give an idea about what this book really refers to, wherever it has used the term 'Hindu Scriptures'.

The following is a short write-up on the main elements of our scriptures, including the specific ones that this book draws majorly from.

Shruti (Vedas and Upanishads)

- Vedas

Nobody knows who wrote the **Vedas**, or how many people wrote them. The Vedas are at least

3,400 years old. While this age of the Vedas is its most conservative estimate agreed to by Western historians, there are enough reasons to consider the Vedas as much older.

The Vedas were passed on from one generation to another by chanting and memorising, for over an absolutely incredible 2,000 years! They were reduced to writing for the first time in 500 CE. That is why they are referred to as Shruti or 'as heard' or 'as revealed'.

It was sage Vyasa who first compiled the vast body of Vedas and classified them under four heads, namely Rig Veda, Yajur Veda, Sama Veda & Atharva Veda

- Rig Veda consists of hymns praising Gods representing different elements of nature, namely water, air, fire, etc.

- Yajur Veda sets out the manner in which the rites and rituals need to be performed. This is more like a manual for the priests.

- Sama Veda explains how the hymns need to be chanted. Sama means melody. It is believed that classical Indian music owes its origins to Sama Veda.

- Atharva Veda is like a manual for the chief priests. It is believed by some that this was a subsequent addition to the other three Vedas.

Each Veda has four sections:

- Samhitas, which set out the hymns that are to be chanted during rituals;

- Brahmanas, which provide the literal meaning of the hymns and a detailed set of instructions for each ritual;

- *Aranyakas*, which interpret the hymns beyond their literal meaning;

- *Upanishads*, which extend the interpretations of **Aranyakas** further to deep philosophical discourses on life, the universe, God, and so on;

Every *Veda* therefore has a

- *Vedapurva*, which are essentially goal-based mantras and rituals, and

- *Vedanta* or *Upanishads*, which dwell on matters of deeper philosophy pertaining to the universe and life;

Another way of classifying Vedas is as *Purva Mimamsa* and *Uttara Mimamsa*, with the former focusing on the rituals, and the latter denoting the philosophy or deeper meaning as espoused in the Upanishads or Vedanta. And since the words '*purva*' and '*uttara*' can also be interpreted as 'early' and 'later' respectively, it could be taken as indicative of the fact that the Upanishads were a later creation and a subsequent addition to the Vedas.

* Upanishads

While the Upanishads or Vedanta are considered by most as a part of the Vedas and the Shruti compositions, they are so special that they merit a special mention. While the rest of the Vedas are in the form of hymns, the Upanishads are stories and conversations between teachers and their pupils on the fundamental questions of life, like:

  * Existence, or otherwise, of God

  * How was this universe created?

  * One's real identity

  * Life's true purpose

  * Is eternal happiness and peace at all possible?

  * What is right and what is wrong in the different situations of conflict that we encounter in our lives, both internal and external?

  * Do we live only once, or is there rebirth?

  * What really happens in and after death?

The creation of the Upanishads has been traced by modern historians to 700 BCE to 1 CE, which is 700 to 1400 years after the period in which the creation of the Vedas has been traced. This may suggest the possibility that the Upanishads were independent creations that got appended to the Vedas subsequently. If this is true, it is quite likely that they were created as a pushback against excessive focus in the Vedas on religious rituals and against social ills like caste-based discrimination that had crept into society. Perhaps that is why the Upanishads state that all creatures are equal and that all of them are manifestations of God, not once but over and over again. The Upanishads also seem to suggest that the Vedas should not always be interpreted literally and the elaborate sacrifices and other rituals detailed in the Vedas were metaphors for the sacrifice of one's ego and for disciplined efforts to evolve oneself.

The Upanishads are the best showcase of the free-thinking spirit that existed in the matters of spirituality and religion amongst ancient Indians. They reflect a spirit of seeking, rather than preaching. Everything is subjected to intense questioning and scrutiny. Nothing, not even the existence of God, has been treated as sacrosanct. That is what makes them riveting, not just engaging. Remarkably, the sages never added their names to these magnificent creations, showing that they were clearly not after personal success, fame, or wealth. Sheer intellectual curiosity and human welfare seem to be the only drivers for this massive and magnificent exercise.

Another aspect of the Upanishads is how our ancient sages seem to have dived so deep into the human mind to understand the different states of human consciousness, several thousand years before psychoanalysis and psychiatry became part of modern science and inquiry. Incidentally, some of the questions dealt with in the Upanishads over 2,500 years ago, like 'What is consciousness'? or 'How did the universe come into being'? are still among the top questions for which man is seeking answers in the internet!

The Upanishads are the backbone of Vedic culture. They have retained their pristine purity due to commentaries on them by greats like Shankaracharya, Ramanujacharya, Madhavacharya, and others. There are many Upanishads, out of which 108 have been commented upon. Ten are of utmost importance.

There are four profound statements (**Mahavakhyas**) in the Upanishads that almost sum up their entire teachings:

1. *Prajnanam* **Brahma** (from Aitareya Upanishad): Consciousness is Brahman

   It is our consciousness that is responsible for whatever we perceive through our sense organs, and our actions. Consciousness is present in every individual. While by itself it does not act or perceive, without it no human function or activity is possible. Like Brahman, it is everywhere and in every being, witnessing everything.

2. *Tat **Tvam asi*** (*Chandogya Upanishad*): That Thou art.

   Here, the teacher describes the nature of the absolute and omnipresent God to the student and then goes on to say that the same absolute and omnipresent God exists within you as your Atman, your real Self, which cannot be destroyed. Therefore, please do not consider yourself separate from God. You are God.

3. *Ayam **Atma Brahma*** (*Mandukya Upanishad*): This Atman (inside us, i.e., our Real Self) is Brahman. In other words, the individual Self or the Atman is no different from Brahman or God. It is a manifestation of God.

4. *Aham **Brahmasmi*** (from *Brihadaranyaka Upanishad*): I am *Brahman*.

   Here, the 'I' stands for the Atman, the spec of God inside us, our witnessing consciousness. This statement inspires every individual to believe that he is complete by himself and there is no need to seek validation from the world.

   All the four Mahavakhyas essentially underline the fact that at our core we are all divine and have everything that is needed for happiness within ourselves. We are all complete by and within ourselves and need no external agent to make us happy and strong.

Smriti

- After Shruti comes the Smriti literature – as embodied in the works of Manu (Manu Smriti), *Yajnavalkya (Yajnavalkya Smriti)*, *Parasara (Parasara Smriti)*, down to the *Tantras*.

- The Smritis have been created by specific individuals, and we know the author in each case.

- The Smritis dwell predominantly on roles and duties of human beings and the rules for engaging within society. Therefore, when interpreting or commenting on Smriti, it is important to bear in mind the context of the times when they were created.

- The Smritis are regarded as subordinate to the Shrutis.

Itihasa

- Under *Itihasa*, we have the two great epics, the Ramayana and the Mahabharata. Many Hindus believe that the events described in these epics did take place in some form and manner, even if not exactly as stated in them.

- If that is true, it is clear that our ancient historians believed in recording history in such a manner that subsequent generations can draw the right lessons from them. Perhaps it was because of this objective that doses of imagination might also have been added to make them more interesting, and the lessons more stark and clear.

- The Ramayana and the Mahabharata introduced the concept of Avatars, wherein it is stated that the Gods themselves descended on earth and lived (and died) as humans, to vanquish evil and restore dharma in society.

- The Mahabharata also contains the Bhagavad Gita, which presents the core essence of the Upanishads in a condensed form.

The Bhagavad Gita

- Out of the 100,000 verses that make up the Mahabharata, the Bhagavad Gita comprises merely 700 odd verses, but they deserve special mention.

The Bhagavad Gita is the most user-friendly presentation of the core Hindu philosophy.

- By explaining the Upanishadic wisdom in the context of a battlefield, the Bhagavad Gita brings out the relevance of this wisdom in our day-to-day lives beautifully. And it presents this content through a conversation between two close friends caught in a sea of conflicts.

- By bringing out the usefulness of our scriptural wisdom so effectively in a practical context, Bhagavad Gita elevates the stature of the core message of Hinduism to great heights. No wonder scores of great men and women from around the world see it as their most trusted guide in life.

Puranas

- Puranas are chronicles containing ancient history, mythology, stories, long and short discourses on religion, philosophy and Yoga.

- The Puranas personify the divine. They are devoted to the exploits and glorification of Vishnu, Shiva, Brahma, Devi, Ganesha, and Skanda.

- Puranas are eighteen in number. The *Vishnupurana, Shivapurana, Bhagavatapurana,* and *Harishchandrapurana* are some of the popular Puranas.

- It is through the Puranas, which present Gods in human forms and settings, that the concept of Personal Gods and idol worship became popular among the Hindus. Therefore, it would be fair to say that the Puranas, more than any other Hindu scriptures, have shaped most of the popular religious beliefs and practises that we see among Hindus today.

Sutras

- The Vedas are too vast. Information on any one topic could be scattered across the Vedas.

- It is the Sutras that first attempted to sort the information under broad and important headings.

- Thus, the Sutras not only compress the Vedas, but also classify and clarify the Vedas by topic.

- There are many Sutras, out of which the following are prominent:
    - *Dharma* Sutra
    - *Grihya* Sutra
    - *Yoga* Sutras
    - *Brahma* Sutra

The Brahma Sutra

- Out of the above Sutras, the Brahma Sutra deserves a special mention.

- Composed by the sage Badrayana, around the start of the common era, the Brahma Sutra has 555 verses.

- It presents the entire wisdom of the Upanishads in a highly structured and scientific manner. It defines God (Brahman), elaborates on the different theories about God, provides a step-by-step process to attain Moksha and become one with God, and also details the benefits of embarking on this journey towards God.

Bhashyas

- *Bhashyas* are commentaries, interpretations and perspectives by scholars on various topics from our scriptures.

- There have been several outstanding *Bhashyakaras* like Adi Shankara, Ramanujacharya, Sayana, or Max Mueller, a Westerner, who has done a Bhashya on Rig Veda.

- You have Bhashyas on every aspect of our scriptures, from Vedas to Itihasa.

There are many more elements and aspects to our infinitely vast scriptures. But the above headings are most significant. It is also widely accepted that in case of any dispute or contradictions between different works in our scriptures, the Shruti literature (Vedas and Upanishads) shall be treated as supreme.

Out of all of the above, the Upanishads, the Brahma Sutras and the Bhagavad Gita are considered the most authoritative and primary sources that teach the means to strive for and attain the ultimate purpose of life. Together, these three are referred to as **Prasthana Traya**. No study of Vedanta is considered complete without an in-depth study of the *Prasthana Traya*.

Unless specifically stated otherwise, the use of the words Shastras, scriptures or texts in this book may be taken to refer to the Upanishads and the Bhagavad Gita.

A Snapshot of the Important Hindu Scriptures:

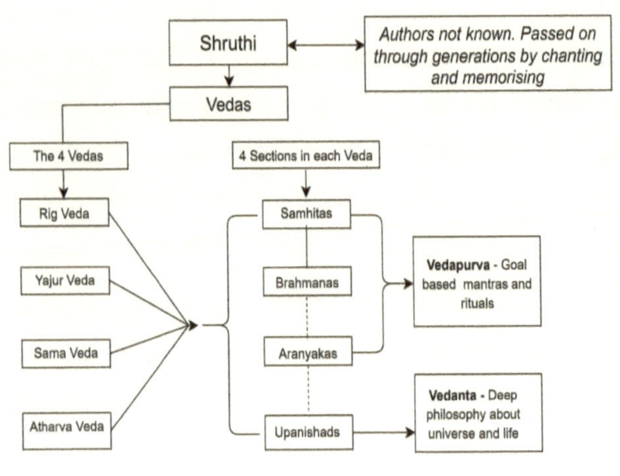

Smriti	Ithihasa	Puranas
Roles and duties of people, and rules for the society	*Epics which many Hindus believe depict history*	*Contain mythology, stories, discourses on religion and philosophy*
Manu Smriti Yajnavalkya Smriti Parasara Smriti and .... others	Ramayana Mahabharata ↓ Bhagavad Gita	18 Puranas, including Vishnu Purana Shiva Purana Bhagavata Purana and others

Sutras	Bhashyas	Prasthana Traya
Classify and clarify Vedas under important topics.	*Commentaries by scholars on various topics from scriptures*	*Most authoritative and primary sources for study of Vedanta*
Prominent ones - Dharma Sutra Grihya Sutra Yoga Sutra Brahma Sutra	Prominent Bhashyakaras: Adi Shankara Ramanujacharya Sayana Max Mueller etc	Upanishads Brahma Sutra Bhagavad Gita

Chapter 31

Acknowledgements & References

Several people have helped me through the journey of this book, and I am truly grateful to all of them. Special thanks are in order:

- To Shri Vishweshwar Hegde (Vishu), an Electronics and Computer Science Engineer with around 40 years of work in organisations like the Indian Institute of Science, Aeronautical Development Agency, Motorola and Mindtree. Currently a partner in PM Power Consulting, Vishu offers leadership development & organisation transformation services to companies. An ardent practitioner of yoga and meditation, Vishu is involved in exploring the application of ancient Indian wisdom & spirituality to modern management, leadership and life at large. Vishu's insights and suggestions have been a constant source of inspiration in this journey.

- To Shri Shivaram AC, a corporate executive, innovator, research scholar and teacher with expertise in Mechanical Engineering, Yoga, Sanskrit, and Ayurveda. With a master's degree in Mechanical Engineering from NIT Surathkal, Shivaram Sir has worked extensively in design and systems engineering at GM, GE, and Applied Materials. Currently pursuing a PhD in Yoga, he is also a visiting faculty at S-Vyasa University, where his engaging lectures inspired me to put together an easily consumable compilation on the subject.

- To Shri Ranga, an IIT and IIM alumnus, a leadership coach for many multinationals for over 25 years and a visiting professor at ISB Hyderabad. Ranga Sir has now undertaken the mission to demystify and simplify Hindu scriptural knowledge and to make it easy for day-to-day application, through an initiative called Joyful Vedanta (joyfulvedanta.org). I was a student in one of the courses offered by this initiative and gained several interesting and invaluable insights from his lectures.

- To my classmate Arvind Sinha, a world-class documentary filmmaker, winner of eight National (President's) awards and several prestigious international awards, and a Sanatani who has done both extensive reading and deep contemplation on the subject. Arvind reviewed my drafts, made some important interventions, and wrote the book's foreword.

- To my ex-colleague Raghavendra Prasad T.S ("Rags"), currently a technology investor, founder of Project StepOne and PassPro Labs, driving healthcare access and startup growth in India. With 25+ years of work in technology and numerous patents, Rags pioneers impactful innovations. A triathlete and philosophy enthusiast, Rags merges passion and purpose in both work and life. Rags reviewed my draft and shared several valuable suggestions, including the one to divide the 31 chapters into broad sections.

- To my ex-colleague Kartik Mishra, an IIT and MIT alumnus, senior executive and founder in India's Tech startup ecosystem, for reading my semi-final draft and providing me with some very imaginative and valuable suggestions to make the family conversation part of the book more engaging.

- To my brother-in-law Mr V V Sundaram, 84, a retired WHO official and an accomplished writer and blogger himself. Mr Sundaram reviewed two iterations of my drafts, and on both occasions effected significant improvements in the language, besides providing me with some excellent suggestions on presentation. He also gifted me with some great books on the subject.

- To my dear friend S Rajagopal, a senior IT professional and a staunch Hindu with knowledge of the Shastras, not just for reviewing my drafts, but also for spending an entire day discussing and debating its contents with me, and in the process providing me with several invaluable inputs.

- To my friends and colleagues (both ex and current) Dattatri Salagame, Rekha Ramaswamy, Bhavin Sheth, Dipen Wahi, Yogesh VB and Siddharth Agarwal, all of whom reviewed my drafts, despite their busy work schedules, and reverted with pointed and valuable inputs.

- To my brother-in-law, Mr P K Venkatramani, retired SBI Chief Manager, who took time off to review my draft over two weeks immediately prior to his only son's marriage and provided me with encouraging feedback from the viewpoint of the rationalist that he is.

- To my colleagues Shashanka Narasimha and Raghuram Mokshagundam for reviewing my draft, providing feedback, and offering valuable suggestions and support.

- To my young colleague, Krupasagar G for his infectious passion for the project. Krupasagar helped me throughout the journey with the flowcharts in the book and in its marketing. Additionally, he connected me with an artiste Sanjay N and coordinated with the later for all the Line Art work in the book.

- To my cousin Sairam, my brother-in-law S. Ramachandran, and my nephew Vineet Iyer for reviewing and commenting on my first summary content, which was in a bullet point format, without the Rajan family conversations track.

- To my dear father-in-law, Shri R S Padmanabhan, 90, who despite his age took the trouble of reading every word of my draft and showered me with his blessings and encouragement.

- Last, but certainly not the least, to my family, my wife Chitra and my two sons Vignesh and Vinayak, all three of whom not just reviewed every draft of the book and provided me with invaluable feedback, but also constantly encouraged me and indulged me throughout this journey with their passionate participation in several debates on the topics and sub-topics covered by this book. Incidentally, Vignesh also did the cover concept and design.

- And finally, my deepest gratitude and respect for the great men of wisdom and the intellectual giants - not only the original creators of our scriptures, but also the great minds that have interpreted, re-interpreted and commented extensively on these masterpieces, making it possible for beginners like me to even attempt understanding the extent of wisdom contained in our eternal dharma.

References

As might well be the case with most modern-day books on the subject, my contribution to this book is more in the nature of compilation as opposed to creating something original. Originality, if any, can be attributed to precious little beyond the selection of the topics, their sequencing, the context setting using a fictional family of four and the language and manner of delivering the message. I owe much of what is stated in the book to what I gathered from some wonderful books, some great podcasts and YouTube videos, some online courses and several discussions with knowledgeable people. The following references merit special mention:

- The Holy Gita: Commentary by Swami Chinmayananda

- The Bhagavad Gita by Shri Nitya Chaitanya Yati.

- Vedanta Treatise by Shri A. Parthasarathy

- Am I a Hindu by Shri Ed. Viswanathan

- Hinduism in the context of Manusmriti, Vedas, and Bhagavad Gita by Shri R. Ramachandran

- The Complete Book of Yoga by Swami Vivekananda

- Kindle Life by Swami Chinmayananda

- The Art of Man-Making by Swami Chinmayananda

- Adi Shankara: Hinduism's Greatest Thinker by Shri Pavan K Varma

- Autobiography of a Yogi by Swami Paramahansa Yogananda

- Dialogues with the Guru - a series of talks with the Late Shankaracharya of Sringeri Sharada Peetham, Sri Chandrasekhara Bharati Swaminah, compiled by Shri R. Krishnaswami Iyer

- The Yoga Instructor Course offered by S-Vyasa University and its study materials

- A compilation of Speeches by the Late Kanchi Shankaracharya, Chandrasekharendra Swamigal

- The online courses offered by 'Joyful Vedanta' and its main teacher, Shri Ranga

- Why I Am a Hindu by Dr Shashi Tharoor

- Bhaja Govindam by Swami Chinmayananda

- Mahabharata by Shri C. Rajagopalachari

- The Vedas and Upanishads by Ms. Roopa Pai

- The Gita by Ms. Roopa Pai

- Hinduism according to Gandhi

- The Bhagavad Gita by Shri Prashant Gupta and Shri M. D. Gupta

- Mahabharata by Shri Kishan Lal Verma

- The study materials of 'Bhagavad Gita - Home Study Course by Swami Dayananda Saraswati'

- Bhagavad Gita, The Song of God, Commentary by Swami Mukundananda

- The website gitajourney.com

- 'My Gita' by Devdutt Patnaik

- Mindfulness at Work by Shri Vishweshwar Hegde

- YouTube videos of Swami Sarvapriyananda of the Ramakrishna Order

- YouTube videos of Sri M, the founder of the Satsang Foundation

Thank You